W9-COT-473

FAULKNER AND THE NEGRO

FAULKNER
and the
NEGRO

by CHARLES H. NILON

The Citadel Press   New York

PS
3511
.A86
Z925

FAULKNER AND THE NEGRO

FAULKNER AND THE NEGRO

I

[William Faulkner's treatment of Negro character is not a separate or distinct aspect of his creation of character. His Negroes, like his other characters, grow from an organic concept of man and of nature. O'Donnell and Cowley have called Faulkner a moralist.[1] His particular moral concept of man's proper relation to man and nature defines and gives shape and outline to his Negro characters.

Throughout the body of Faulkner's stories, there is found a very definite social theory, predicated upon certain clearly articulated moral assumptions about the land and the people of his fictional world. The theory is one which seeks to understand the present through a detailed knowledge of the past and which tests the hypothesis that present evils grew from past evils. This theory is of necessity historical because the evils which beset the present grew from man's attempts to possess the land, a violation, according to Faulkner, of God's intention.]

Isaac McCaslin affirms the evil of attempting to own land when he tries, by giving up to his cousin the land which is his legal inheritance, to rid himself of the inherited sin of his fathers.[2] "I can't repudiate it [Isaac says]. It was never mine to repudiate. It was never father's and uncle Buddy's to bequeath to me because it was never grandfather's to bequeath to them to bequeath to me to repudiate because it was never old Ikemotubbe's to sell for bequeathment and repudiation".[3] The land could not be bought:

Because he told in the Book how He created the earth, made it and looked at it and said it was all right, and then He made man. . . . He created man to be His overseer on the earth and to hold suzerainty over the earth and the animals on it in His name, not to hold for himself and his descendants inviolable title forever, generation after generation, to oblongs and squares of the earth, but to hold the earth mutual and intact in the communal anonymity of brotherhood, and all the fee He asked was pity and humility and sufferance and endurance and sweat of his face for bread.[4]

In addition to this attempt to own the land, which Isaac finds to be a violation of God's intentions, the white man had bought slaves to till it for him. Slavery was a denial of "the communal anonymity of brotherhood", a perversion per-

---

[1] Malcolm Cowley, "William Faulkner's Legend of the South", in *A Southern Vanguard*, ed. Allen Tate (New York, 1947), pp. 13–27; George Marion O'Donnell, "Faulkner's Mythology", *Kenyon Review*, I (Winter 1939), 284–299.

[2] William Faulkner, "The Bear", *Go Down, Moses* (New York, 1942), pp. 256–263.

[3] *Ibid.*, p. 256.

[4] *Ibid.*, p. 257.

1

mitting that humankind be made into an instrument to secure material gain. Slavery denied the white man the opportunity of "pity and humility and sufferance and endurance and sweat of his face for bread". Isaac McCaslin describes slavery as "the general and condoned injustice and its slow amortization, but the specific tragedy which had not been condoned and could never be amortized".[5]

The responsibility for these two, almost twin, evils is man's; for the truth that is not clear from the Bible is found in man's heart.[6] The truth of the heart triumphs over interpretation.[7] From Faulkner's point of view, man's will is free: "God created and man himself cursed and tainted".[8] In "Delta Autumn" Faulkner says:

He put them both here: man and the game he would follow and kill, foreknowing it. I believe He said, "So be it". I reckon he even foreknew the end. But He said, "I will give him his chance. I will give him warning and foreknowledge too, along with the desire to follow and the power to stay. The woods and fields he ravages and the game he devastates will be the consequence and signature of his crime and guilt, and his punishment".[9]

The two evils are very often the determinants of Faulkner's character portraits. At the outset, it should be said that as a rule Faulkner does not develop character. He reveals it. Frequently, he reveals it by showing how the evils affect a particular individual, or how, as is often true of the Negro, individuals avoid the effects of the evils. Evil is a destructive agent. Faulkner's Negroes survive. His stories about Negroes illustrate the means and define the nature of their survival. This entails showing the qualities or virtues that may overcome evil, or establishing a point of view toward evil.

If Faulkner's work is examined as a whole, an optimistic point of view can be found. He says, as a matter of fact, "There are good men everywhere, at all times. Most men are. Some are just unlucky, because most men are a little better than their circumstances give them a chance to be. And I've known some that even the circumstances couldn't stop".[10] The details with which Faulkner makes his principles clear are frequently pessimistic and ugly, but the principles are not. He says that quality is not "is", but "does".[11] He urges that man must not seek to escape the responsibility of his humanity. His cardinal virtues are pity, humility, sufferance, endurance, and sweat. To these Cowley adds a love of justice and a love of liberty.[12] Faulkner admires the

---

[5] Ibid., p. 266.
[6] Ibid., p. 260.
[7] Ibid., pp. 260–261.
[8] Ibid.
[9] "Delta Autumn", Go Down, Moses, p. 349.
[10] Ibid., p. 345.
[11] William Faulkner, "There Was a Queen", Doctor Martino (New York, 1942), pp. 98–119.
[12] Malcolm Cowley, The Portable Faulkner (New York, 1946), p. 19.

individual but not the social being.[13] Essentially, Faulkner's principles are moral ideas that relate to the formulations, evaluations, and decisions that man must make in society. Lionel Trilling describes these ideas as a piety — not a religion — "but he [Faulkner] wishes to suggest religion, as piety inevitably must".[14]

The two evils that Faulkner recognizes have not remained on the level of fact but have been active forces in the making and shaping of Yoknapatawpha County. Through their operations the Indians were destroyed; the prominent families, Sartoris, Compson, Benbow, Sutpen, McCaslin, grew and declined; the Snopeses came, prospered, and declined; and the Negroes endured.

Faulkner's good people recognized the evil in their world. They were not without insight, but with the exception of the McCaslins and Miss Habershams, they seem powerless to make choices of good or evil. Cowley says their code did not allow them to fight the forces of evil.[15] The Snopeses, who come into the county, represent not necessarily a new evil but an evolution and reinforcement of the old. Their guiding principle is a crass materialism, a scientific methodology which by some critics is thought to symbolize the post-Civil War and continuing attempts of the industrial North to foist its way of life upon the South.

The effects of the two evils, according to Faulkner, have not all been harmful. The South did produce a particular kind of society which, while it was dependent upon certain evils, had certain virtues. As a region, it possessed the virtue of a tradition; as a people, it possessed homogeneity. Although the South has been powerless to correct its evils, it has not been unaware of them. Faulkner, the moralist, believes that the South must, and in time will, rid itself of the evils, and at the same time that it can and will save the democratic promise of the nation. The evil which Faulkner's social theory presents is derived from a misuse of power. Federal intervention to correct social evils in the South would, from Faulkner's point of view, also involve the use of power, a use which he thinks would continue the evils that should be destroyed.

[13] Mark Schorer, "The Novel and the Individual", *Kenyon Review*, XII (Spring 1950), 357–358. Schorer makes use in these pages of a criticism made by D. H. Lawrence of the characters of John Galsworthy. "Why can't we admit them as human beings?" Lawrence asks. His answer reflects Faulkner's attitude toward the individual and the social being: "It is because they seem to us to have lost caste as human beings, and to have sunk to the level of the social being, that peculiar creature that takes the place in our civilization of the slave in the old civilizations. The human individual is a queer animal, always changing. But the fatal change today is the collapse from the psychology of the free human individual into the psychology of the social being, just as the fatal change in the past was a collapse from the freeman's psyche to the psyche of the slave. The free moral, and the slave moral, the human moral and the social moral: these are the abiding antitheses".

[14] Lionel Trilling, "Contemporary American Literature in Its Relation to Ideas", *American Quarterly*, I (Fall 1949), 206.

[15] *The Portable Faulkner*, pp. 14–17.

4

The South must, therefore, solve its own problems; and when it has solved those, it must save the other sections of the country.[16]

The body of social theory basic to an understanding of Faulkner's white and Negro characters and to a knowledge of his attitude toward the South and its relation to the nation as a whole is given its most complete summary in *Intruder in the Dust*. The plot of this novel provides a metaphorical statement of the thesis. Gavin Stevens, who is a point-of-view character, gives an explicit analysis of it.[17]

Within the novel there is a set of symbols that function almost allegorically. Old Man Gowrie is the composite of the obtuse, God-fearing, "nigger-hating" poor white of the backwoods Mississippi counties. The twins, his sons, Vardaman and Bilbo (the use of these names is intentional) are the national representatives of people like Old Man Gowrie. Like his sons, the Vardamans and Bilbos are twins in intention. Faulkner implies that such men are controlled by people like Old Man Gowrie. By further implication it might be judged that getting rid of the real Vardamans and Bilbos is an ineffective gesture, unless something is done about Old Man Gowrie. The difference in the dress of the twins may be taken to indicate the superficiality of the difference in Vardaman and Bilbo. Faulkner is not kind to the twins. They are lesser men than their father, who has the beak of an eagle.

The twins are made the instruments of the novel's thesis, which Stevens explains. They represent the white South proving to itself that the Negro is not guilty of injury to it and voluntarily treating him justly. That is, the Gowrie twins open the grave of the dead Gowrie and discover its secret. Old Man Gowrie refuses to allow the prisoners, who were the tools of the law and in a sense outsiders, to open the grave. The twins discover that it is empty. The white people of the South discover their own dilemma.

Old Man Gowrie represents man against odds. Nature, his sterile barren hillside home, conspires against him and forces him to break the social code in order to live. Except in Beat Four, his home community, he is a social outcast. He is the poor white gone to the dogs. His tragedy is that he has not escaped being human. He has a family. Paradoxically, he has religion and God. He loves and hates and fears. Though his sons are worthless, they are his; and when one of them is killed, he must grieve and wish to kill in return. He has the prejudices of the poor white. He realizes as Sutpen did that he has less status in the community than a favored Negro servant. Being human and weak, he blames the Negro for most of the evils of his condition. When the Negro (he thinks) becomes the instrument of the death of his son, all of

[16] William Faulkner, *Intruder in the Dust* (New York, 1948), pp. 145-155.
[17] *Ibid.*

his fury and hate are unleashed. His honor is at stake, and he must avenge the injury to keep his self-respect and his respectability. It is ironic that a man like him should have honor and respectability.

Old Man Gowrie observes decorum. He buries his son from the church at Caledonia, and then he hopes to get revenge and end the affair. But there are complications which increase the stature of his character and gain the reader's sympathy for him. They testify to his membership in the vulnerable human family. The poise, control, and firmness that he has when he comes upon Hope Hampton, the sheriff, preparing to open his son's grave, are brought into sharp contrast when he discovers that his son's body has been taken from the grave and buried in the quicksand of the creek bed. The passion of his love for his son is seen in his frantic recovery of the body. At the end of this action the reader is again impressed with the strength of the man. Hope tries to avoid telling him that Vinson, the dead Gowrie, has been murdered by his brother Crawford. But the old man will not accept this kindness. He absorbs the full shock of the truth. Composed and containing his grief, he tells the twins, "All right, sons. Let's load our boy on the mule and take him home".[18]

The dead Gowrie may be taken as the death of the promise of the old South, or as the death of that South. Lucas is the Negro who is accused of destroying the South, and he has become the factor that motivates its conscious action. That is, Lucas is a descendant of slaves. The institution of slavery was begun to enable the white man to keep and profit from the land. Symbolically, the legally free Negro must represent the evolution of the evils that were unleashed by the South upon itself. The lynching that threatens Lucas may represent the effort of the South to avenge its loss and to save what is left of its past. In the minds of many Southerners, Lucas is mistaken for the evil he represents. By punishing Lucas many people feel that the doom of the South can be averted. That Lucas, who is thought by many to be the cause of the South's impending doom, can be at the same time the conscience that directs the South to examine itself is evidence of a dualism. The will to punish Lucas is not separate from a sense of injustice to him.

When the grave of the old South, the grave of the Gowrie son, is opened, it is discovered that the death of the old South had not been caused by Lucas, but by a white man. In effect, it had killed itself. Materialism had, in a sense, been the instrument of the death. Because of Lucas's force as the South's moral conscience, this discovery is made through a plan of action that he suggests. When Old Man Gowrie and the twins, Vardaman and Bilbo, make the same discovery, they realize that they must assume the burden of their guilt. They take the body of the murdered son home and do what they can with it. Their

[18] *Ibid.*, p. 179.

action suggests that the South can and must assume the responsibility for the evil that it has brought upon itself.

This metaphorical representation of the social theory of *Intruder in the Dust* may be somewhat forced, but it has the virtue of suggesting that Faulkner has been interested in the society of his world as a whole rather than in a particular situation. The factors, however, that make the particular action or conduct of the plot possible are the factors that distinguish the Faulkner society from the larger society — the Nation. The thesis of the novel is intended to clarify morally the position of this region in regard to its racial particularity; not that the racial particularity is the whole of its distinction from the North, East, and West, but that it is symbolic of that distinction. Faulkner argues that the homogeneity of the region is its main distinction. Racial injustice is not essential to the survival of the region. In fact, it will and must go. But the white people of the South must destroy it. They must not have a pattern superimposed upon them. Their pattern must evolve from their past. The actions of Charles Mallison, Miss Habersham, and the local representatives of the law, and the speeches of Gavin Stevens show how this can be done.

Faulkner's world is a society of men who think it an advantage to live in a traditional way, and who believe that man fulfills his nature and reaches his proper stature in such a situation. Although it may seem a contradiction, his society cherishes intelligence, amenity, and tolerance, and has the courage necessary to support these virtues. His society has flexibility and modulation. A code of honor is central to it, and demands that it uphold justice and continuity. This society believes that it can change itself gradually by taking thought and revising sensibility. The standards of the society are passed on by men through their children. In it men have respect for God and the dead and solicitude for the unborn. This can be seen in the force and vitality of the past as it operates in the present and presages the future. This is the thesis of *Intruder in the Dust.*

The particular constitution of the society of the South (the thesis) is made clear in the novel in several ways. The Gowrie family is:

a connection of brawlers and farmers and fox-hunters and stock- and timber-traders who would not even be the last anywhere to let one of its number be killed by anyone but only among the last since it in its turn was integrated and interlocked and intermarried with other brawlers and fox-hunters and whiskeymakers not even into a simple clan or tribe but a race a species which before now had made their hill stronghold good against the country and the federal government too, which did not even simply inhabit nor had merely corrupted but had translated and transmogrified that whole region....[19]

[19] *Ibid.*, pp. 35–36.

Stevens tells his nephew, Charles Mallison, that the Gowries do not attach a great deal of importance to death and dying; but they put "a lot of stock in the dead and how they died".[20]

The jail which housed Lucas was old, brick, square, proportioned, "built in a time when people took time to build even jails with grace and care".[21] It is this jail that the architect from the city admires. He tries to buy its hand-hewn door. Not only is he fascinated by the jail but by the whole town. He recognizes that it has something which the city does not have. The solidity and genuineness of the door are symbolic of that.

Frequently the description is related to the past in such a way as to show that the society's roots are there. When Miss Habersham was being driven to the jail to sit on its ancient porch and give her white woman's protection to Lucas, she passed "old big decaying wooden houses of Jefferson's long-ago foundation ... which even when children lived in them seemed still to be spellbound by the shades of women, old women still spinsters and widows waiting even seventy-five years later for the slow telegraph to bring them news of Tennessee and Virginia and Pennsylvania battles".[22] These old houses are in contrast to the "day-after-tomorrow shoulders of the neat small new one-storey houses designed in Florida and California".[23] Faulkner does not like the new houses. They are essentially mean. A whole subdivision is now built in what twenty-five years ago had been considered small for a front lawn. The new houses presupposed an inferior way of life:

where the prosperous young married couples lived with two children each and (as soon as they could afford it) an automobile each and the memberships in the country club and the bridge clubs and the junior rotary and chamber of commerce and the patented electric gadgets for cooking and freezing and cleaning and the neat trim colored maids in frilled caps to run them and talk to one another over the telephone from house to house while the wives in sandals and pants and painted toenails puffed lipstick-stained cigarettes over shopping bags in the chain groceries and drugstores.[24]

Details of this sort are not essential to the plot of this novel, but they amplify the thesis.

In a sense, Faulkner may be said always to establish a relation between man, his environment, and the past. The structure of his writing usually reveals his effort to establish this relation. His people, their land, and their history are always inseparable. Because of this the structure of a Faulkner

---

[20] *Ibid.*, p. 66.
[21] *Ibid.*, pp.49-50. The first section of *Requiem for a Nun* describes this same jail. Faulkner uses the jail as a symbol for and as an index to an understanding of all of the events in the county.
[22] *Ibid.*, pp. 119-120.
[23] *Ibid.*
[24] *Ibid.*

novel or story is a means of revealing character. It is perhaps of value to give a detailed analysis of a Faulkner passage here to show how character is revealed through the structural unification of man, nature, and history.

For several reasons, chapter seven of *Intruder in the Dust* is suitable for this purpose. Faulkner is not concerned with revealing the character of a Negro in this chapter, but that is unimportant because his method of character portrayal does not differ for his white and Negro characters. In this chapter, it can be assumed that Charles Mallison's character is being revealed to him. Like many other Faulkner characters, he is in search of self-knowledge or self-identification. By understanding the things around him, Charles learns what he is; and in the same way, the reader learns what and who Charles is. Charles does not develop. He is, and Faulkner tells us why.

The chapter begins with Charles and his uncle driving behind Hope Hampton's car on their way to open again the Gowrie grave. The chapter ends with the discovery that the grave is empty. This is the final proof that Lucas is not the murderer. Chapter seven begins with movement, a kind of processional from Jefferson to the Gowrie grave, intent upon formally proving Lucas's innocence. It is a Monday morning, May ninth, before noon. Charles has not slept since Friday night. The motion of the car might be expected to put him to sleep, but it does not. His mind moves as the car moves, and he is conscious of his need to complete his understanding of his region and to complete his acceptance of his responsibility in that region. The ride from Jefferson to the Caledonia churchyard is for him a ceremonial rite, a kind of initiation. The speed of his mental processes alters with the speed of the car and the change of the natural scene. He sees the beauties of the land. There are flowers and fields. He sees the ugliness. There are the Negro cabins, with their unkept yards, closed on this particular day and apparently lifeless. Their seeming emptiness and desertion symbolize the fact that not just Lucas is awaiting his fate, but that all of the Negroes in the county are awaiting that same fate.

Charles remembers that Aleck Sander and Paralee, Aleck's mother, are the only Negroes he has seen since Lucas was made a prisoner. At the moment of this realization, in the wide expanse of an empty field, he sees a Negro plowing. He stares at the Negro, and the Negro stares at him — "the man and the mule and the wooden plow which coupled them furious and solitary, fixed and without progress in the earth, leaning terrifically against nothing". This brief glimpse was a part of the ritual. Just as remembering the faces of the mob that peered at him through the windows of the car as they left the town was part of it. Somehow he had to relate the land, the mob, and the figure of the plowing Negro. The speed of the car increases, and the natural scenery changes.

The texture and organization of the chapter so far are interesting. There is Charles's youthful annoyance at not being able to sleep, at not being able to step out of the situation at the point at which he is. He has proved Lucas innocent. He should be able to stop there, to sleep. He cannot. The memory of the faces in the mob makes him aware of this. The natural beauty of the land and the contrasting ugliness of the life upon it are forced into his consciousness. The human factors are framed by natural factors. Charles's thinking is blocked-out for him by the natural scene.

As Gavin Stevens increases the speed of the car, the scene changes, the pine covered hill replacing the furrowed fields. Charles begins to think again. His thought is a remembering of something that his uncle has told him at some time in the past. It is an explanation of the relation of the people to the land. He seems to remember each word of the speech and for the first time to understand its meaning. The ceremonial quality of this ride is preserved when Gavin Stevens interrupts Charles's thought process and begins to speak. To Charles, it was as though the speech might be a continuation of the one his uncle had made long before in the past.

The scene changes, and the "willow-and-cypress bottom of the Nine-Mile branch" is visible. Stevens explains the character of the people who live in this section in terms of the nature of the land. The reader becomes aware that Stevens's talk is a speech and not just conversation, when Charles interrupts him to tell him where to turn off; and he says he knows and continues. Up to that point he has discussed two segments of the region's population, people like the Gowries and more prosperous, more respectable farmers. He next discusses the Negro whom, in the aggregate, he calls Sambo. There has been the physical contrast of the barren hills and of the fertile valleys. Sambo, Stevens says, can live in both.

Following this passage, there is one of natural description. So far in this chapter, Charles's thinking has modulated into his uncle's talking. The drive has only been a starting point for conversation. At the end of Stevens's speech, it is possible to realize that the local situation is not the central problem in his mind. Stevens, whose attitudes we must take as the author's, is concerned with the whole South and its relation to the nation. For the first time, with the mention of the atomic bomb, we realize how close Stevens is to the present.

Charles is again aware of the natural scenery — "and now he seemed to see his whole native land". The ceremonial continues, and Charles, who is being initiated, sees himself as a part of a specific tradition, a tradition stemming from the earth. He sees himself special and unique. His particularity is emphasized for him through his realization of his relation to, and his oneness with, the mob whose "conglomerate" face had peered at him earlier in the morning through the windows of his uncle's car. As Charles thinks, his home unfolds beneath him like a map. Nature and the earth are used in a special way. Charles realizes that they have ordained the way of life in this region. The Mississippi is "the great River itself flowing not merely from the north but out of the North circumscribing an outland — the umbilicus of America joining the soil which was his home to the parent which three generations ago it had failed in blood to repudiate".

The reader begins at this point to realize that Charles has become a projection of Stevens. He is thinking what Stevens might have said if he had kept talking. It is as if as a result of the ritual, the spirit of Stevens, for a while, is dwelling in Charles. Faulkner's thesis is unfolding. Already he has defined the South as a particular geographical region whose geography has determined a specific race.

Now he examines the relation of the Southerner to the North. The North was a region that Charles had been emotionally conditioned not to accept. He could see it only as "the massed unaccountable faces". As he thinks of it, his uncle speaks and explains why he cannot break his separateness from the North. "It's because we alone in the United States ... are a homogeneous people". Faulkner expands this thesis. The South is not resisting progress. It is not defending its political way of life but its homogeneity from "a federal government to which in simple desperation the rest of this country has had to surrender voluntarily more and more of its personal and private liberty in order to continue to afford the United States". Faulkner evidently intends the plot of the novel to illustrate the homogeneity of the region. "We (I mean all of Us: Beat Four will be unable to sleep at night until it has cancelled Lucas Beauchamp ((or some one else)) against Vinson Gowrie in the same color of ink, and Beat One and Two and Three and Five who on heatless principle intend to see that Beat Four makes that cancellation.)" This unity of action and thought comes from a homogeneous people. Faulkner says it is essential to literature, art, science, and freedom and that it is the most valuable characteristic in a time of crisis.

The focus of Stevens's speech then shifts to Sambo: "the postulate that Sambo is a human being living in a free country and hence must be free". Stevens argues that the South must free Sambo because the North cannot. He finds the Negro homogeneous too, "except that part of him which is trying to escape not even into the best of the white race but into the second best".

Again there is a shift from Stevens's talk to Charles's thinking. They have arrived at the cemetery. Instead of nature framing the end of Stevens's speech, a description of the church is given. The church stood "asking nothing of any, making compromise with none and he [Charles] remembered the tall slender

spires which said Peace and the squatter utilitarian belfries which said ⸜
and he remembered one which even said Beware but this one said sim↳
Burn". The image of the church and its meaning reinforce Stevens's argumen↳.
Like the church, the people of the South would be intractable and independent.

The progression in this chapter is made through certain stylistic devices, mainly interpolations and parenthetical discussions. To achieve these, the dash, the colon, parentheses, and italics are used. Occasionally the beginning of a new sentence indicates the beginning of a new block of thought or a shift of point of view. Conversation in the chapter, and in the whole book for that matter, is usually not more than an exchange of a few sentences. These are usually short. Sometimes, they form the substance around which other blocks of stream-of-consciousness exposition are given. Faulkner's technique seems often to be one of narration by exposition and frequently, almost totally in this novel, his technique is expository. In this chapter, conversation before the church is reached serves purposes of transition. It does not narrate or explain. The third person telling of the story permits Faulkner to manipulate his characters, and when the stream of consciousness assumes first person intimacy and closeness, he can adjust the focus by the use of the third person. The use of this person also provides another means of transition. In this chapter several segments of the story are blocked out in this fashion. The first sentence of the chapter begins "They never saw". The next thought passage begins "They were going faster", and the next "They could see the hills". When the church is reached the sentence begins "Now they were there".

The sentences that begin with matter-of-fact third person statements usually call the reader's attention to the physical presence of the characters in relation to the scene. This is usually followed by a rather poetic nature description and progresses to a description of something that man has grafted on the land or to a consideration of man's relation to the earth. The end of such passages is likely to contain an abstraction or a generalization. Then the pattern is repeated. In this chapter there are four such sections.

Within the sections or blocks of thought, progression and variety are achieved through the use of the dash, colon, parenthesis, italics, conversation. Usually the sentences are long, but, after reading Faulkner for a time, it becomes apparent that the colon and semicolon may be almost conventionally regarded as full stops. The dash and the parentheses are used to break a thought that is to be completed after Faulkner has qualified it or given it the proper setting. The very long sentences are frequently broken into paragraphs. A colon usually marks the suspension of thought. Such breaks occur in no regular fashion: sometimes before conversation, sometimes when an indirect quotation is being used. The use of the dash and parentheses makes

aulkner to prolong almost indefinitely the sentence in which
ed. Italics are used primarily to achieve emphasis or to indi-
aracter is thinking rather than remembering. Although this
ier self-conscious, it is distinctive texturally.

At the church, the plot begins to unwind itself again. The sheriff has come to open the grave and verify the information which Charles and the others gave him. His task is complicated by the appearance of Old Man Gowrie and the twins, Vardaman and Bilbo. The complication is overcome, and the grave is opened and found to be empty.

As the structure of this chapter can be related to the revelation of Charles Mallison's character, so structure in Faulkner's stories can be related to the portrayal of his other characters.

Faulkner establishes a relationship between the people and the land. The sparse hills on which the Gowries live resemble the Scottish highlands from which their ancestors came. On the hills there are the Gowries, Frasers, and Worketts (who were really Urquharts but whose ancestors could not spell), and in the valleys along the river were the people named Littlejohn, Greenleaf, Armstead, and Millingham, and Bookwright. Sambo, the Negro, lived in both places, because he could stand anything.[25] Charles Mallison was conscious of "the dirt, the earth which had bred his bones and those of his fathers for six generations".[26] The past was shaping him into a specific man with specific passions, part of a "race specific and unique".

II

Lucas, who is Faulkner's definitive portrait of the Negro, was not one of the new folks. He says, "I belong to the old lot. I'm a McCaslin".[27] Lucas is an individual rather than a social being. His quality is defined by what he does rather than by what he is. He possesses Faulkner's cardinal virtues and accepts his own humanity.

Because Lucas is given the place he has in the plot of *Intruder in the Dust*, it is proper, perhaps necessary, to ask to what extent his status depends upon his mixed blood. In so far as white blood means a particular biological inheritance that contributes superior intelligence, Faulkner suggests that there is none. He suggests that racial differences are superficial, that largely they are social and economic differences or psychological differences which derive from mental states produced by these.[28] Miss Rosa Coldfield becomes aware of this

[25] *Ibid.*, p. 149.
[26] *Ibid.*, p. 151.
[27] *Ibid.*, p. 19.
[28] William Faulkner, *Absalom, Absalom!* (New York, 1936), pp. 97, 136–137, 139, 317–318.

in *Absalom* when Clytie stops her from climbing a stair by touching her.[29] At the moment when Clytie's hand is against her body she knows that flesh is flesh.[30] At that moment, she is aware that her social knowledge is only social knowledge. Circumstances affect this knowledge, so that in their cooperative struggle for survival against natural forces, Rosa, Judith, and Clytie are just three women; the social distinctions of race are no longer functional.

In *The Unvanquished*, Bayard defines the nature of race, "Ringo and I had been born in the same month and had both fed at the same breast and had slept together and eaten for so long that Ringo called Granny Granny just like I did, until maybe he wasn't a nigger anymore or maybe I wasn't a white boy anymore".[31] In another passage, Bayard say "That's how Ringo and I were. We were almost the same age, and father had always said Ringo was a little smarter than I was, but that didn't count with us, anymore than the difference in the color of our skins counted. What counted was what one of us had done or seen that the other had not".[32] Later in his life Bayard says, "Father was right; he was smarter than me".[33] In this instance a white person is admitting that a Negro whose blood is not mixed is intellectually his superior. In "The Bear" there is the long passage in which Isaac McCaslin talks to Roth Edmonds about the children of Ham. It is in this passage that he says, "they are better than we are".[34]

It is true that Lucas says he belongs "to the old ones — I'm a McCaslin". But in this instance Faulkner seems to be referring to family and tradition in a social sense and not to be suggesting that *being* a McCaslin makes one superior, but rather that *doing* what McCaslins do makes one superior. To say that he is a McCaslin is to state Lucas's homegeneity, to affirm the source of his particular moral code. The question of the importance of Lucas's white blood may be handled in this way.

Lucas's story is told in "The Bear", "The Fire on the Hearth", "Go Down, Moses", and *Intruder in the Dust*. Lucas is a product of the McCaslin conscience: their sensing of guilt, their recognition of evil, and their effort to atone for and to repair the harm they had done. He is, in fact, a continuation of McCaslin morality applied in the social category of the Negro.

In "The Bear", Lucas's story is told through Isaac McCaslin's reactions to the content of a set of ledgers that had been kept by his father and his uncle. The entries to which the reader's attention is called record the vital statistics

[29] *Ibid.*
[30] *Ibid.*
[31] William Faulkner, *The Unvanquished* (New York, 1938), p. 7.
[32] *Ibid.*, p. 91.
[33] *Ibid.*, p. 142.
[34] "The Bear", p. 294.

of the slaves the family had owned. Frequently, the entries are abbreviated and not complete. Isaac reacts to each fragment as his eyes move down the pages, and through his interior monologues, composed of memories, speculations, sensations, and analyses, he gives the ledger entries full meaning. The technique is one of importance; for it reveals Faulkner's belief that there is something more than that which meets the eye in the human situation, that the facts alone are not enough. Faulkner separates the facts, and the physical separation is a technique that gives value to the facts and character to the person who forms their subject. Through the facts from the ledgers, the reader learns more than Lucas's origin.

Lucas's grandmother, when a slave girl, was taken into her owner's home and into his bed. This action causes her mother to drown herself. The ledger entry at this point reads "Who in Hell ever heard of a nigger drowning himself?"[35] From his memories, Isaac recreates the scene and the explanation: "he seemed to see her actually walking into the icy creek on that Christmas day six months before her daughter's and her lover's (*Her first lover's* he thought. *Her first.*) child was born, solitary, inflexible, griefless, ceremonial, in formal and succinct repudiation of grief and despair who had already to repudiate belief and hope".[36] Before this passage we learn through Isaac's thinking that it is possible that the girl was old Carothers McCaslin's daughter. This knowledge, the question in the ledger, and Isaac's visual image of the woman give a full picture. The question in the ledger presents the conventional stereotype of the Negro as an insensitive and unfeeling being. The knowledge that Carothers seduces a girl who may be his own daughter, with full knowledge of this fact, defines his particular moral depravity. But Faulkner does not allow the act to represent moral depravity alone. Isaac McCaslin seeks through his own sensitivity and knowledge of human nature for some further motive, for some human, and therefore redeeming, motive for his grandfather's act.

The act as Faulkner presents it is essentially repulsive. Carothers is an old man, with middle-aged sons. Perhaps, Isaac thinks, Carothers sent for the girl out of loneliness. He had shown the girl's family respect of a kind by going to New Orleans to purchase her mother as a wife for her father, a favored slave. Isaac is not willing to see his grandfather's act primarily as an act of lust and power. In his mind he insists: "*But there must have been love he thought. Some sort of love. Even what he* [Carothers] *would have called love: not just an afternoon's or a night's spittoon*".[37]

[35] *Ibid.*, p. 267.
[36] *Ibid.*, p. 271.
[37] *Ibid.*, p. 270.

This attempt to determine Carothers's motivations seems important not only as a means of understanding Lucas's origin, but as a significant insight into Faulkner's attitude toward miscegenation. When the quoted passage in the paragraph above is read, the passage from *Absalom, Absalom!* in which Rosa talks of the effect of Clytie's touch upon her should be remembered:

I know only that my entire being seemed to run at blind full tilt into something monstrous and immobile, with a shocking impact too soon and too quick to be mere amazement and outrage at that black arresting and untimorous hand on my white woman's flesh. Because there is something in the touch of flesh with flesh which abrogates, cuts sharp and straight across the devious intricate channels of decorous ordering, which enemies and lovers know because it makes them both — touch and touch of that which is the citadel of the central I-am's private own: not spirit, soul; the liquorish and unguarded mind is anyone's to take in any darkened hallway of this earthly tenement. But let flesh touch with flesh, and watch the fall of all the eggshell shibboleths of caste and color too.[38]

Isaac, no doubt, believes that his grandfather gained a similar knowledge of human relations.

Such knowledge may be responsible for Carothers's effort to assume some responsibility for his acts. When Lucas's father, Tomey's Turl, was born, Carothers entered in his will that Tomey's Turl was to receive a thousand dollars when he was twenty-one. Faulkner's comment on this attempted assumption of responsibility shows the acuteness of the problem that Carothers faced. Carothers made:

no effort either to explain or obfuscate the thousand-dollar legacy to the son of an unmarried slave-girl, to be paid only at the child's coming-of-age, bearing the consequence of the act of which there was still no definite incontrovertible proof that he acknowledged, not out of his own substance but penalising his sons with it, charging them a cash forfeit on the accident of their own paternity; not even a bribe for silence toward his own fame since his fame would suffer only after he was no longer present to defend it, flinging almost contemptuously, as he might cast-off a hat or pair of shoes, the thousand dollars which could have no more reality to him under those conditions than it would have to the negro, the slave who would not even see it until he came of age.... *So I* [Isaac] *reckon that was cheaper than saying My son to a nigger he thought.*[39]

Tomey's Turl did not claim the legacy his father left him, but he did continue the black McCaslin line by adding three children to it. Lucas was the youngest of these. Rather than divide their father's legacy equally between the three descendants, Carothers's sons, Buck and Buddy, in an effort to deal honestly by their black nephews, provide that each of them is to receive a thousand dollars when he is twenty-one. It becomes Isaac's responsibility to see that this is done.

[38] *Absalom, Absalom!*, p. 79.
[39] The Bear", p. 269.

Isaac tries harder to escape the evils of the misuse of the land and slavery than the earlier McCaslins had. He relinquishes his claim to the McCaslin land to his cousin McCaslin Edmonds in consideration for fifty dollars a month for the remainder of his life. His final act of relinquishment and atonement, too, for that is what he hopes his action is, is the effort to provide in some way for his family's Negro descendants. So it is that he keeps the legacy for Lucas, whose origins he has tried to interpret and put into a frame of reference, in trust until he is twenty-one.

When Isaac relinquishes the land, much of his thinking is about the Negro. In "The Bear" this thinking represents Faulkner's attitude toward Negroes as a group.[40] It is of importance in understanding Lucas, because Lucas embodies its ideal. When Isaac and his cousin, who is to receive his birthright, talk of their grandfather's motivation for leaving Lucas's father, and, through him, Lucas a patrimony, Isaac insists "He didn't want to. He had to. Because they will endure. They are better than we are. Stronger than we are. Their vices are vices aped from whitemen or that whitemen and bondage have taught them: improvidence and intemperance and evasion — not laziness: of that white men had set them to, not for their aggrandisement or even comfort but his own".[41] The virtues and vices of Faulkner's Negro characters are summarized in this passage. If Lucas is Faulkner's Negro embodiment of these, we must not expect him to be a perfect man. He is to have virtues and vices.

Lucas and other Faulkner Negroes are, in effect, illustrative in function. They do not, however, like Miss Glasgow's Negroes, illustrate a Negro myth. If Faulkner creates a mythology at all, it is meant to be a human mythology. His Negroes are human beings; "only in the surface matters of food and clothing and daily occupation" are the white characters "any different from the negro slaves who supported them — the same sweat, the only difference being that on the one hand it went for labor in the fields".[42] Lucas can sell whiskey, lie, and steal and not have these things referred to as peculiar to Negroes and as indications that Negroes are different from white people.

Lucas is an individual rather than a social being; the things he does are important; and he assumes the responsibility of his humanity. Perhaps all of these can be summed up in his statement "I'm a McCaslin". In "The Fire on the Hearth", Faulkner makes these virtues concrete. Interestingly enough, the story develops two episodes from Lucas's life on the Edmonds plantation, where he has had granted him for life a house and ten acres to work as he pleases. These episodes concern a still and a divining machine, a mechanism

[40] *Ibid.*, pp. 260–315.
[41] *Ibid.*, pp. 294–295.
[42] *Absalom, Absalom!*, pp. 97–98.

designed to aid in the discovery of buried gold. At the outset, it can be said that it is just like a "nigger" to run a still and to believe in finding buried money. Lucas operates his illicit distillery for twenty years. His mania to find gold drives his aging wife to seek a divorce and almost results in her death. In the two situations there is a stereotyped surface versimilitude, and it is through them that a casual effort in the direction of plot is established. The technique used in working out the plot situations is somewhat ratiocinative in nature. Discovery and evasion are interrelated to reveal the quality and working of Lucas's mind. Evasion is a technique of survival, and through it we see how Lucas keeps ahead of the two white men. The surprise elements in Lucas's small victories amuse the reader and make Lucas understandable.

Paradoxically, these two situations that reveal Lucas's mental agility and craftiness also reveal his greed. Lucas wants to possess the land; he wants money. That is why he violates the law of the state to sell liquor. That is why he endangers his union with his wife. Lucas is an old man. He has to his credit in the bank more money, perhaps, than his landlord, Roth Edmonds, has. He does not need money. His desire for it is the effect of the evils that man has brought upon the land. The quality of Lucas's survival is not free from the taint of the sin of his region. But Lucas is an individual. He is an individual in the sense that he is not a "nigger".

Through the use of flashbacks and stream-of-consciousness monologues that fragment the two rather conventional episodes of this story, a kind of delving beneath the surface, Faulkner shows us the making of Lucas into an individual. In doing this there is a juxtaposition of events in time that almost merges the past and the present. Lucas is sixty when the story takes place, and Faulkner narrates the details of these two episodes, informing and giving them the accumulated meaning of Lucas's whole life.

In Lucas's life there is a series of positive actions, doings, which show him to be an individual. He goes to Isaac McCaslin and asks for his patrimony. "Will the bank keep it for a black man same as for a white?" Lucas asked Isaac. And Isaac said, "I will ask them to".[43] So at twenty-one Lucas Beauchamp is a man with money in the bank. The year is 1896, and he goes to work for Mr. Zack Edmonds on the plantation where he was born. His decision to remain in the South is a positive action that indicates Lucas's conscious acceptance of himself as a Negro. He does not attempt to escape his humanity, as a flight to another section of the country might have symbolized. Lucas establishes a home and begets a child. The fire that he builds on his hearth, and which burns more than forty years, is symbolic of the meaning of home to him.

[43] "The Bear", p. 257.

The crucial event in Lucas's life occurs when he takes his wife back from Zack Edmonds. Lucas's boy was born six months before Edmonds's was. Edmonds's wife died when her child was born, and Edmonds took Mollie Beauchamp and her child to live in his house and to be more than a wet nurse for the baby, Roth. The things Lucas does when he becomes aware of his wife's relation to Edmonds, and the methods Faulkner uses to reveal his character are significant. The details of this struggle are given in the second section of the first division of the story. Zack Edmonds is dead and his son, who is grown, lives in his house. Lucas has gone to Roth Edmonds's house in an effort to protect his still from discovery. When Roth answers Lucas's knock on his door, the sight of him causes Lucas to remember a visit he made to the house when Roth's father was alive. Through a flashback, Faulkner reconstructs this earlier visit. The past action began when Lucas went to Zack Edmonds and said, "I wants my wife. I needs her at home".[44] Following Zack's protest Lucas says: "I'm a nigger. . . . But I'm a man too. I'm more than just a man. The same thing made my pappy that made your grandmaw. I'm going to take her back".[45] The statement indicates the operation of a code in Lucas's life. The question of what is to be done to Edmonds after his wife is returned is gone over by Lucas in his mind. *"I will have to kill him, he thought, or I will have to take her and go away".*[46]

Quite a struggle took place in Lucas's mind the night that Mollie returned to their cabin:

Maybe when he got old he would become resigned to it, but he knew he would never, even if he got to be a hundred and forgot her face and name and the white man's and his too. *I will have to kill him,* he thought, *or I will have to take her and go away.* For an instant he thought of going to the white man and telling him that they were leaving, now, tonight, at once. *Only if I were to see him again right now, I might kill him, he thought. I think I have decided which I am going to do, but if I was to see him, meet him, now my mind might change — And that's a man! he thought. He keeps her in the house with him six months and I don't do nothing; he sends her back to me and I kills him. It would be like I had done said aloud to the whole world that he never sent her back because I told him to but he give her back to me because he was tired of her.*[47]

Thoughts of his home, the burning fire, the fence that gave privacy and of the order and peace that had been part of his life before the white child was born filled Lucas's mind, and he thought, "Why she aint even knowed unto right now that I even suspected".[48] He watched Mollie suckle the white child before the hearth and asked "Whar's ourn? . . . Whar's mine"? Mollie prepared to

[44] "The Fire on the Hearth", *Go Down, Moses,* pp. 46–47.
[45] *Ibid.,* p. 48.
[46] *Ibid.,* p. 47.
[47] *Ibid.*
[48] *Ibid.*

take the white child back to his father's house, but Lucas stopped her: "I went to Zack Edmond's house and asked him for my wife. Let him come to my house and ask me for his son".[49] Zack Edmonds did not come and Lucas took his razor and went to Zack's house to kill him. In Zack Edmonds's bedroom he threw the razor away, and the two men struggled for Edmonds's gun. Neither man did physical injury to the other, but an understanding and a bond of respect developed between them. "You thought that because I am a nigger I wouldn't even mind", Lucas said. *I was wrong, the white man thought. I have gone too far*".[50]

Lucas decides to act in order to protect his honor. He expects his action to result in his being lynched.[51] But he is willing to accept the consequences of his action in order to do what Carothers McCaslin would have wanted him to do.[52] A part of what Lucas means when he says he is a McCaslin is that he accepts the morality of the McCaslins. Lucas says, as the physical struggle between Edmonds and him begins, "All you got to beat is me. I got to beat old Carothers".[53] In this instance Lucas is more of a traditional man than Zack Edmonds.

As Lucas begins the fight, Faulkner describes him as statuesque, larger than life, a heroic figure. Zack Edmonds sees his foreshortened chest with the faded shirt stretched across it. The logic that Lucas maintains during the encounter is not realistic. The effect is as though there were two of Lucas, one engaged in mortal combat and the other observing from a distance, commenting, evaluating, unmoved, certain of the outcome of the struggle. A misfire prevents Lucas from killing Edmonds and the struggle continues, but Lucas's stream of consciousness shifts and the reader is not given the details that marked the end of the struggle. Lucas's action has been positive. He has rejected the easy solution. His action has not been predicated upon a knowledge of outcomes or prescribed by a regard for safety. The fact that his action has not been consistent with his knowledge of the world is affirmed in the questions that he asks himself at the end of this flashback: " 'How to God', he said, 'can a black man ask a white man to please not lay down with his black wife? And even if he could ask it, how to God can the white man promise he wont? ' "[54] This question poses the paradox of the ideal and the real. The fact that Lucas can ask such a question, and that his past has been what it is, prevents the reader from judging him according to the level of the stereotype of the Negro and the still.

[49] *Ibid.*, p. 50.
[50] *Ibid.*, p. 55.
[51] *Ibid.*, p. 53.
[52] *Ibid.*
[53] *Ibid.*
[54] *Ibid.*, p. 59.

In the next section of the story the reader's attention is brought back to the present and to Lucas's effort to prevent the discovery of his still, and to prevent his soon-to-be son-in-law from going into business and competing against him. The second episode in this section of the story shows Lucas dealing with the problem of evil. He is human and accepts his humanity. Human weakness brought the two evils upon the South. Other McCaslins had fallen before these evils, and so does Lucas. Lucas falls and, like the other McCaslins, recognizes, atones for, and tries to correct his wrong. In this section of the story Lucas is a man possessed and driven by some inner urge. In this respect he is typical of Faulkner's heroes. His possession resembles that of Sutpen or Sartoris men. He does not sleep at night, nor does he work his fields during the day. His wish to discover buried treasure consumes all of his energies. While he is possessed by it, he is a kind of superman who overcomes all of the obstacles that get in his way.

In this section of "The Fire on the Hearth", the central events are the purchase of the divining machine, the theft of a mule, Mollie's unrest and decision to divorce Lucas, the outwitting of Roth Edmonds (Zack's son), and the machine salesman, and finally Lucas's realization of the enormity of his wrong. In this, as well as in the still episode, we are aware of Lucas's craftiness, and resourcefulness and of the ratiocinative quality of his mind. He is able to turn his defeats into victories. In effect he forces Roth to pay for the divining machine. When he doubts that he will find money, he craftily inspires the salesman with his own greed and uses him for his own ends. Lucas's basic understanding of human nature and his ability to direct and use it for his own ends is one of his most distinctive characteristics.

The question of how Faulkner reveals Lucas's character is partially answered through the use Lucas makes of other people and through the attitude other people take toward Lucas. This is essentially a method of analogy in which the height of the hills is determined by examining the depths of the lowlands. Lucas's stature can be measured in terms of the stature of the obstacles that he overcomes. Roth Edmonds and the galaxy of Southern conventions are not mean adversaries. Sometimes Lucas is characterized through the use of psychic distance. Such a method involves the use of physical distance between the character and the person who observes him as a means of enlarging the character's stature. An example of the use of psychic distance to reveal Lucas's character is seen at the end of the court scene when Lucas has decided not to allow Mollie to divorce him.[55] Mollie and Roth are in Roth's car and Roth thinks that Lucas is getting in. Instead of joining them, Lucas tells Roth to wait:

"Wait a minute?" Edmonds said. "Hah!" he said. "You've bankrupted your waiting.

[55] *Ibid.*, p. 129.

You've already spent —". But Lucas had gone on. And Edmonds waited. He stood beside the car and watched Lucas cross the square, toward the stores, erect beneath the old, fine, well-cared-for hat walking with that unswerving and dignified deliberation which ever now and then, and with something sharp at the heart, Edmonds recognized as having come from his own ancestry too as the hat had come. [The hat had been given to Lucas by old Carothers.] He was not gone long. He returned unhurried, and got into the car.[56]

Roth is forced to wait and is forced to observe. The car is his; the ground, in fact, on which Lucas lives and earns his living, since it belongs to Lucas by law only as long as Lucas lives, is Roth's. Roth should call the tunes, but he does not. And as Lucas moves away from the waiting car, psychologically, through a focusing of the facts the reader already knows, the separation by distance of the two men contributes to a revelation of Lucas's character.

In the quotation above Roth notices a hat that Lucas wears. This hat, like Miss Habersham's shoes and gloves, is one of the "things" that enables us to recognize Lucas and his particular quality.[57] Faulkner uses things as a symbolic means of characterization. His admirable people have a taste for "things" that are not shoddy. Lucas cherishes several articles that were given to him by his grandfather — a handsome beaver hat, a gold toothpick, a gold watch and chain. Lucas also wears, when he goes to town, "threadbare mohair trousers such as Grover Cleveland or President Taft might have worn in the summertime".[58] Frequently, these prized possessions seem to represent a peculiar kind of eccentricity in their owner. Except for Miss Habersham's thirty-dollar shoes and eighteen-dollar gloves, her dress is that of the poor white. The items of Miss Habersham's dress are used to establish her character. Her round black hat that sits on the top of her head, her gold watch suspended from her neck, her eighteen-dollar gloves and her thirty-dollar shoes reveal her strength and her attitudes toward life. They are compatible with her driving her own truck and earning her own living. Bayard Sartoris wore jeans that cost a dollar and a half, but his boots were expensive and handmade for him.[59] Usually Faulkner gives the cost of "things", and some significance must be attached to their being very expensive or very cheap. Some suggestion of what Faulkner hopes to gain through his use of "things" is seen in his handling of the five-cent straw hat that Sam Fathers habitually wears.[60] This hat, before Sam went to live in the woods, was what the Negro cotton picker usually wore and was the badge of his social inferiority. In the woods it became a symbol of Sam's dignity.[61]

The statement "I'm a McCaslin" suggests that Lucas will do the things

[56] *Ibid.*
[57] *Intruder in the Dust*, p. 157.
[58] "The Fire on the Hearth", p. 97.
[59] William Faulkner, *Sartoris* (New York, 1929), p. 200.
[60] "The Bear", p. 199.
[61] *Ibid.* See also "The Old People", *Go Down, Moses.*

that McCaslins do and that his tastes are those of McCaslins. Lucas strives to be like his grandfather. The hat, the trousers — the "things" are a sort of bodying forth of the man. They do not make the man, but they represent him. They establish his connection with a particular past; they symbolize a particular set of values.

Lucas's attitude toward things is a direct contrast to Sutpen's. Sutpen erroneously hopes to create himself through possessions. Through the use of things, Sutpen tries to become something he is not, tries to escape the burden of his humanity, fails to achieve pride and humility.[62] The "things" that are associated with Lucas do no harm to others. This is not true of Sutpen's possessions. Sutpen's effort to escape his humanity causes him to treat others inhumanely, to make instruments of them. This is illustrated in his efforts to get the fine marble tombstones home to his Hundred during the heat of the Civil war.[63]

Lucas, however, is not free from the taint that destroys Sutpen. He does have a desire for possessions that is different from his possession of things. His greed for money leads him to treat other men inhumanely, and it is his recognition of this that causes him to abandon his search for buried money. He attempts to make Edmonds pay for the divining machine. When Edmonds refuses to pay, he steals and uses one of Edmonds's mules as payment. When his theft is discovered and Edmonds insists that the mule be returned, Lucas takes advantage of the greed of the salesman and through this advantage makes the salesman an instrument for his own purposes. During the period of Lucas's obsession, he fails in his discharge of his responsibility to his wife.

The nature of the evil that possesses Lucas is defined by his wife. This evil is an aspect of the two evils that have cursed the South. Mollie's statement of it, though mixed with a superstitious fear which in part defines and gives her character a surface reality, clarifies the nature of the abstraction. Mollie says that Lucas is crazy, that he is doing a thing the Lord did not "mean for" folks to do:[64] "Because God say, 'what's rendered to my earth it belong to Me unto I resurrect it. And let him or her touch it, and beware'. And I'm afraid. I got to go. I got to be free of him".[65] Mollie not only recognizes the effect of the machine upon Lucas, but she is also aware of the effect it will have upon others. Lucas says he will give it to George Wilkins, his son-in-law, but Mollie objects: " 'No!' she cried ...! Not that he [Lucas] would keep on using it just the same as if he had kept it, but he would fetch onto Nat, my last one, the curse of God that's gonter destroy him or her that touches whats

[62] *Absalom, Absalom!*, pp. 8, 12–13, 79, 156.
[63] *Ibid.*, p. 220.
[64] *Ibid.*, pp. 101–102.
[65] *Ibid.*, p. 102.

done been rendered back to Him".[66] Mollie insists upon having a divorce. This insistence for the second time threatens the fire that burns on Lucas's hearth. It is this threat that brings him to his senses.

The use of the machine is a commentary on Faulkner's method of handling his Negro characters. The machine itself is an incarnation of the evil influences of materialism, scientific methodology, utility divorced from function, that has descended upon the South. Mollie's recognition of the machine's evil nature, and Lucas's escape from its influence, are an illustration of the Negro's survival. Lucas escapes and survives; Sutpen is trapped and destroyed. The use of the machine also shows that Faulkner treats his Negro characters in the same way that he does his white characters. This single basis of treatment is an indication that, in an absolute sense, Faulkner recognizes the oneness of humanity.

The search for buried money shows Lucas bearing the burden of his humanity and, in the end, making a right choice. This episode, like that of the still, does not concern itself primarily with the present. In the still episode, it is Lucas who remembers the past, reconstructs it, and through it enables the reader to appreciate him and his relation to Roth Edmonds. In the machine episode, Roth Edmonds is the point-of-view character. It is through him that we have Lucas's actions interpreted. Here again Faulkner uses the principle of under-cutting. Roth has status which is acknowledged. If he evaluates Lucas as his superior, psychologically the reader is willing to accept his judgment. Faulkner's technique resembles, at this point, that used by Henry James.[67] Roth becomes a kind of reflector. Faulkner examines in Roth's mind, during the development of the machine episode, most of the facts of Lucas's life, including those events that Lucas and Zack Edmonds, Roth's father, were involved in. This near-repetition of facts serves to give emphasis and a coherent outline to Lucas's character.

Roth Edmonds's approach to Lucas is through his sympathy for Mollie, who was the only mother he ever knew.[68] He accepts Lucas's affront to Mollie as an affront to himself and sees it not as a single event, but as one of a pattern of events that he reconstructs. He generalizes first on Lucas's relation to the McCaslin lines; then he reconstructs a chronology of events, interpolating and interpreting them, that as a whole shows Lucas's dominance among the members of the McCaslin line.[69]

[66] *Ibid.*, p. 122.
[67] Joseph Warren Beach, "Introduction". Henry James, *The American*, Rinehart Editions (New York, 1949) , pp. ix-x.
[68] "The Fire on the Hearth", p. 104.
[69] *Ibid.*, pp. 104–131.

Through Roth, it is pointed out that Lucas's character is not dependent upon the mixture of his blood:

It was as if he were not only impervious to that blood, he was indifferent to it. He didn't even have to bother to defy it. He resisted it simply by being the composite of the two races which made him, simply by possessing it. Instead of being at once the battleground and victim of the two strains, he was a vessel, durable, ancestryless, nonconductive, in which the toxin and anti stalemated one another, seetheless, unrumored in the outside air. . . .[70]

Roth contrasts Lucas to his brother and sister who left Mississippi, who tried to escape. "But Lucas remained. He didn't have to stay".[71] Then he tells of Lucas's marrying and begetting a child and of his own relation to Lucas's family; of his final realization that he was white and different from Lucas's son who was his playmate.

Roth began as a child to recognize that Lucas did not behave toward his father as other Negroes did. As a boy Roth spoke to his father about this. He thought then that there must have been something between his father and Lucas, and when he grew older, he discovered what it was:

My father and a nigger, over a woman. My father and a nigger man over a nigger woman, because he simply declined even to realize that, had even refused to think *a white woman.* He didn't even think Mollie's name. That didn't matter. *And by God Lucas beat him,* he thought. *Edmonds,* he thought, harshly and viciously. *Edmonds. Even a nigger McCaslin is a better man, better than all of us. . . . Yes, Lucas beat him, else Lucas wouldn't be here. If father had beat Lucas, he couldn't have let Lucas stay here even to forgive him. It will only be Lucas who could have because Lucas is impervious to anybody, even to forgiving them, even to harming them.*[72]

Roth's examination of his relationship to Lucas, Mollie's power to evoke the past in his mind, provides an understanding of Faulkner's method and helps to establish Lucas's meaning when he says "I'm a McCaslin".

Mollie's visit to Roth is a means of affirming that "Lucas is impervious to anybody, even to harming them". The passage also provides some motivation for Edmonds's attempting to help Mollie. Helping Mollie was a way of helping Lucas.[73] The power that Lucas had gained over Zack made Roth aware of Lucas's power over him.

In "The Bear" and "The Fire on the Hearth", Lucas is a particular person acting under the force of particular circumstances. As a person in *Intruder in the Dust*, Lucas is not active. He motivates the other characters to act.

[70] *Ibid.*, p . 104.
[71] *Ibid.*, p. 105.
[72] *Ibid.*, pp. 115–226.
[73] *Ibid.*, pp. 116–117.

Lucas, the man, in this story is very much like the concept of him that Roth Edmonds presents near the end of "The Fire on the Hearth":

He's more like old Carothers than all the rest of us put together, including old Carothers. He is both heir and prototype simultaneously of all the geography and climate and biology which sired old Carothers and all the rest of us and our kind, myriad, countless, faceless, even nameless now except himself who fathered himself, intact, complete, contemptuous, as old Carothers must have been, of all blood black white yellow or red, including his own.[74]

Faulkner says of Lucas that he is tyrant over the whole country's white conscience. In *Intruder in the Dust*, through the various reactions toward Lucas and his supposed crime, Faulkner reveals the attitudes of Southern white people toward Negroes.

As a whole, *Intruder in the Dust* may be regarded as not adding to the character of Lucas, but of being an additional affirmation of it, a part of and belonging with the Lucas of "The Bear" and "The Fire on the Hearth". Here again the Jamesian technique of providing a number of windows through which a character may be seen is used. Lucas, as a visible person, is seldom seen in the novel; as a felt or pervasive influence he determines the entire action. The story opens with Charles Mallison, part of a crowd, waiting on a Sunday morning for the sheriff, Hope Hampton, to deliver Lucas to the security of the jail in Jefferson. It ends with Charles Mallison and his uncle, Gavin Stevens, waiting for and finally serving Lucas's wishes.[75] As a participant in the action of the story, Lucas is seldom seen. While he is in jail in Jefferson he is visited by Charles and Stevens. He is seen again on the night when the trap is set to catch Crawford Gowrie, the real murderer. Whenever they are important to the story, his actions, past or present, are reported. The relation that existed between Charles Mallison and him is reported. The real and supposed events that circumstantially related Lucas to the death of Vinson Gowrie are reported. Throughout the novel, people talk about Lucas. The total effect of seeing Lucas, of having his actions reported, and of having his actions commented upon, does present a portait. It is essentially the portrait of a man who is so complete that he is above mere human undoing, a man who is intractable, who wins the reader's admiration, but does not need his sympathy. The reader cannot suffer with him because he does not suffer. In *Intruder in the Dust*, Lucas wins no victories like the one with Zack Edmonds. He is a symbolic figure, and the reader must accept the symbol as Faulkner interprets it through the characters who perform the action of the story. Lucas is a kind of abstraction that generates and sets in motion without being

[74] *Ibid.*, p. 118.
[75] *Intruder in the Dust*, pp. 235–247.

changed itself, a moral goad pricking and urging the white conscience of Jefferson and the entire county.

The plot of this novel develops around Lucas. It is believed that he shot and killed Vinson Gowrie. He is placed in jail in Jefferson, but it is believed that the people from Beat Four, the community of the dead man, will take him from the jail and lynch him. The lynching is prevented by Charles Mallison, a sixteen-year-old white boy who feels that he owes a debt to Lucas; by Miss Habersham, a spinster lady whose servant Lucas's wife had been; and through their use and direction of the agencies of the law. Charles met Lucas first when he was hunting on the Edmonds plantation. He fell into a creek and was taken into Lucas's house so that his clothes might dry. When the clothes were dry, Lucas gave him a meal. Charles was twelve years old when this happened, but he was conscious of what was proper behavior for a white person when he had received a service from a Negro. He offered Lucas the coins that he had in his pockets, and Lucas refused them: "What's that for? the man said, not even moving, not even tilting his face downward to look at what was on his palm: for another eternity and only the hot dead moveless blood until at last he could bear the shame: and watched his palm turn over not flinging the coins but spurning them downward ringing onto the bare floor".[76] At Lucas's command Aleck Sander, Charles's Negro playmate, picked the coins up and returned them to him.[77] After this, Charles goes hunting for rabbits, but he thinks of Lucas: "We got to make him be a nigger first. He's got to admit he's a nigger. Then maybe we will accept him as he seems to intend to be accepted".[78] Charles is twelve years old when this happens, but he does not forget the incident. For a time, paying Lucas becomes an obsession with him. He gives Lucas tobacco for himself and snuff for his wife in his first effort to pay his debt. Then he gives Lucas's wife a gaudy silk dress. The gifts are designed to obligate Lucas and to make him act like a "nigger". Shortly after the gifts are received, Lucas sends Charles a gallon of syrup by a white boy who brings it riding a mule. Charles thought "it was even worse this time because Lucas had commanded a white hand to pick up his money and give it back to him. . . . This would have to be all; whatever would or could set him free was beyond not merely his reach but even his ken; he could only wait for it if it came and do without it if it didn't".[79] He did not try to pay the debt again. He began, not without questioning and doubt, to accept his responsibility to Lucas. This assumption of responsibility and its discharge form the shape of the story.

[76] Ibid., pp. 15–16.
[77] Ibid., p. 16.
[78] Ibid., p. 18.
[79] Ibid., pp. 22–23.

The story begins with Charles watching the jail so that he can see Lucas when Hope Hampton takes him there for safe-keeping. The plot is both comic and grotesque. It is fantastic to think that a young white boy can save a Negro from a lynch mob. Charles's debate with himself, his sparring with Lucas and losing to him, his plans which finally include Aleck Sander and Miss Eunice Habersham, all contain a large element of fantasy. Although the fantasy has the chastening support of the Christian ideal that a child shall lead them, it is paradoxical; and in the world of statistics and documented social fact, it is comic. The actions which make the progression of the plot are grotesque. After chapter four, in which Lucas literally commands Charles to assume responsibility, the plot ceases to be merely comic, because it is not entirely plausible, and becomes grotesque because of actions that are incongruous when judged in the context of modern life. The laughter that the plot inspires is always the ironic laughter of disbelief. It is difficult to believe that an old Negro man could make white people do the things that are done in this novel. Faulkner insists that the events of the story be accepted, in their significance at least, as true to life. In *Absalom, Absalom!* and in *Light in August*, there is an aesthetic distance that does not make this necessary. In *Intruder in the Dust*, the thesis destroys aesthetic distance and forces the reader to judge all the materials of the story in terms of reality. The elements of the plot are not unusual Faulkner elements, and without the thesis the story might succeed almost as well as other Faulkner stories do. Lucas does not weld the disparate elements of the story into a unity, because he is the subject of the story rather than a character in the story. Lucas must remain untouched and unchanged to prove the thesis; and so the actions set in motion to save him, since he determined them and set them in motion, seem a little like a game that he is playing for his own amusement. Therefore the reader's emotional involvement with the plot comes not so much from the impact of Lucas's character as it does from the impact of ideas about the situation that Lucas represents.

Lucas as a concept inspires an idealism. It is this idealism, this moral attitude toward evil, that motivates the action of the novel. The contrived and grotesque aspects of the actions and of the settings emphasize the moral intention of the good characters. Miss Habersham, Charles Mallison, Hope Hampton, Gavin Stevens (the good characters), Aleck Sander and a truck, a horse, funeral sprays and a grave, an unidentified rider, and the dark of the night are an incongruous group. Faulkner puts Edmonds, who would normally be expected to defend Lucas, in a hospital in New Orleans, and the men in Charles's family do not believe his suggestions that Lucas is innocent. This makes it inevitable that Charles and the others should assemble at the graveside as Lucas had directed. The inevitability is contrived and the resulting actions are grotesquely comic, but through this contrived inevitability the moral idealism of the good characters is made evident and the status of Lucas as an abstraction is defined. This is a paradox of the comic ideal.

It is paradoxical that a Negro like Lucas should have lived seventy-five years in a world like his. Faulkner stresses the paradox of Lucas's being alive after he was taken by the law. This paradox he widens and explains by the introduction of another. Beat Four would not lynch Lucas while he was in the custody of its law-enforcing agent. This illustrates the Southern attitude toward law and the Negro. Beat Four respected its own unit of the law; however, when Hope Hampton, the county sheriff, had taken Lucas away and placed him in the county jail, he became fair prey. This attitude toward authority is essentially that of the supporters of States' Rights toward the Federal Government. An enlargement of this attitude is seen when the elements of the other beats of the county do not lynch Lucas after he is brought into Jefferson by the sheriff. They would help, but the responsibility and the privilege of doing the lynching belonged to Beat Four. There is an element of sentiment here. This paradoxical etiquette is also illustrated in the lynching of Rider ("Pantaloon in Black").

This oblique attitude toward the law is continued in the conversation between Gavin Stevens and the jailer when Stevens goes to visit Lucas. The jailer says to Stevens:

So you got to get mixed up in it too. You can't let well enough alone neither.... Don't mind me. I'm going to do the best I can; I taken an oath of office too.... But don't think nobody's going to make me admit I like it. I got a wife and two children; what good am I going to be to them if I get myself killed protecting a goddamn stinking nigger.... And how am I going to live with myself if I let a passel of no good sonabitches take a prisoner away from me?[80]

The jailer's attitude is placed in perspective by the attitude of Will Legate, who is a special deputy hired for Lucas's protection. When asked about resisting the mob if it should attempt to take Lucas, Legate says: "Oh I got to.... Mr. Hampton's paying me five dollars for it".[81] The attitudes of the three men are placed in a context of sentiment by the truth of the situation which all of the agents of the law agree to. That is, if the mob decides to lynch Lucas, the law cannot prevent them. These paradoxes indicate that pride, which is a

---

[80] *Ibid.*, p. 53. Many of the critical responses to Lucas (in *Intruder in the Dust*) suggest that he seems larger than he really is. Alfred Kazin's (*On Native Grounds*, New York, 1942, p. 459) comment on this tendency is valuable: "Significant has been his [Faulkner's] need to represent almost all his characters at the unwavering pitch of absolute desperation and damnation, to expand everything to a size larger than life and ambiguously more tragic, to represent everything — every life, every thought, every action — as something unutterably lost and doomed".

[81] *Ibid.*

growth from sentiment, rather than the law itself is the element of stability and order in the town. The functional law which stems from the *mores* of the past is reflected in Mr. Lilley, the grocer, and made explicit in Stevens's explanation of him:

He has nothing against what he calls niggers. If you ask him he will probably tell you he likes them even better than some white folks he knows and he will believe it.... All he requires is that they act like niggers. Which is what Lucas is doing: blew his top and murdered a white man — which Mr. Lilley is probably convinced all Negroes want to do — and now the white people will take him out and burn him, all regular and in order and themselves acting exactly as he is convinced Lucas would wish them to act: like white folks; both of them observing implicitly the rules: the nigger acting like a nigger and the white folks acting like white folks and no real hard feelings on either side.... Which proves again how no man can cause more grief than that one clinging blindly to the views of his ancestors.[82]

Hope Hampton is in a rather crucial position. He must carry out the laws of the society and the laws of the federal government. His position is somewhat like Zeus's in one of Lucian's satires when he finds himself expected to answer prayers for rain and for fair weather all in the same moment. The view of Hampton's position shows the particular social and psychological complexity of Faulkner's region. Faulkner says Hope handles his situations by going slow and breathing hard. This going slow and breathing hard actually amounts to interpreting and applying the law in terms of the folkways peculiar to the region, and being concerned finally with end results and not processes. Hope captures Crawford Gowrie in this manner and allows him to commit suicide. This strategy protects him and protects the Gowrie family. It is a courtesy to them and increases their obligation to Hope.

There are other paradoxes in the novel that reveal white attitudes toward Lucas as an abstraction. One of the most ironic of these is that the symbol of white womanhood guards Lucas. Lucas is thought to have injured white womanhood. (A murderer injures a mother by indirection.) When Miss Habersham and Charles's mother, mending their laundry, sit on the porch of the jail, they are saying in effect that the whole symbolic structure around which bi-racial living coheres in the South is false. This is ironic; for, if they are inviolable, their men cannot show them disrespect to get Lucas. If they reject the protection that their men offer (if they say, in effect, as Miss Habersham was doing, that they did not need to be protected from the Negro) then the symbol is broken and the men are frustrated. Erskine Caldwell has such a scene at the end of *Trouble in July*. In his situation the men have completed the lynch ritual and are ready to leave the scene, when the woman whose honor they have avenged stands before the victim's body and denies that her

[82] *Ibid.*, p. 48.

honor has been injured. For a moment the men are helpless. She has made their action completely meaningless, revealed them to themselves as brutes, invalidated their code. In their helplessness, they acknowledge her as their greatest enemy, revert to the brute, and this time in self-defense, stone her until she is dead. The force of this paradox is strengthened by Christian symbolism. A jail is in effect a tomb, but Lucas is no longer in this tomb. He has been apotheosized. If the men of the community ask, Miss Habersham can say: "He is risen as he said". The symbolism is true in a double sense. Miss Habersham knows that Lucas did not kill Vinson Gowrie. In that sense he is risen. And although she does not know it, Lucas is not in the jail. Hope Hampton was not sure that a mob could be controlled by the fiction of a white woman's impregnability. He had taken the precaution of hiding Lucas in his own home.

Lucas is an example of Faulkner's moving from the particular to the general in Negro characterization. At first Lucas is a person and then he becomes a symbol for a race. The creation of his character historically and socially, and the use that Faulkner makes of him in *Intruder in the Dust*, support the contention that Faulkner is primarily a moralist and that his Negro characters are consistent with his moral theory and dependent upon that theory for their particular existence.

Faulkner's social theory and Lucas Beauchamp have been treated in some detail because the two together seem essential to an understanding of Faulkner's Negro characters. The smaller portraits of the other novels and stories, in effect, say what Lucas says or develop some aspect of Lucas's meaning. The remainder of this essay may be called progress toward Lucas Beauchamp; for, although *Intruder in the Dust*, in which Faulkner accords Lucas a kind of apotheosis, is not Faulkner's best novel, or aesthetically his most satisfying treatment of the Negro problem, Lucas is his most definitive portrait and judgment of the Negro.

There is a fairly large group of Faulkner stories in which the mention or presence of Negroes is merely incidental. Among these are "Barn Burning", "The Hound", "The Fox Hunt", "Dr. Martino", "Lo!", "A Courtship", "A Rose for Emily", and four of the stories in *Knight's Gambit*—"Smoke", "Monk", "Tomorrow", and the title story.

The Negro characters and references to Negroes in these stories contribute to the verisimilitude of time and place. Many times these Negroes exist outside of or in addition to the central plot structure of the stories, but in spite of their limited function they contribute to an understanding of Faulkner's treatment of Negro character. In all of the stories listed above, the effects of the twin evils upon the Negro can be seen and their survival is predicated.

In "Barn Burning", for example, Snopes sends his messages by a "strange nigger", and it is that fact rather than the ominous message the Negro brings that is commented on in the town.[83] The watchful air of Major de Spain's Negro butler is a folk attitude of the Negro that reveals his character and gives some understanding of the group to which he belongs. He says, "Wipe yo foots, white man, fo you come in here; Major de Spain ain't home nowhow".[84] This direction reveals his attitude to Snopes and to his employer. Snopes's "Get out of my way nigger" reflects his side of the antagonism.[85] When Snopes has a message to send to Major de Spain, his young son says: "Ain't you going to even send a nigger? At least you sent a nigger before".[86] The child shows in his remark an understanding of status and place, as well as a knowledge of the evil that his father is about to do. Faulkner reveals the Negro's attitude toward morally ambiguous situations in a brief episode in "Hands Upon the Water".[87] Late at night, Gavin Stevens goes to a Negro cabin for information. A voice answers his call and knock, but no light shows. Then a woman's voice is heard to say, "You come away and let them white folks alone"![88] The caution is similar to that of the de Spain butler who watches the Snopeses from behind a curtain before he lets them enter the de Spain home. Of the Negro woman's caution Faulkner says: "Almost always, there is in Negroes an instinct not for evil but to recognize evil at once when it exists".[89] To some extent, "The Hound" illustrates this.

In "The Hound", Faulkner uses folk attitudes to show how Negroes are regarded by white people. The murderer in the story has heard that a dog would howl at the grave of his master. His comment on this possible fact is "Nigger talk".[90] In connection with this reaction Faulkner gives, as he often does, a direct explanation of the character's behavior. Of the murderer he says, "(he had never known a Negro himself, because of the antipathy, the economic jealousy, between his kind and the Negro's)".[91] At the end of the story the white murderer is put in a cell across from a group of Negroes who work on the chain gang, and who were in jail for vagrancy "or for selling a little whiskey or for shooting craps for ten or fifteen cents".[92] When the Negroes are fed before he is, the murderer complains: "Are they going to feed them niggers before they feed a white man?"[93] It is not possible to say that

[83] William Faulkner, "Barn Burning", *Collected Stories* (New York, 1950), p. 4.
[84] *Ibid.*, p. 11.
[85] *Ibid.*, p. 21.
[86] *Ibid.*
[87] William Faulkner, "Hand Upon the Waters", *Knight's Gambit* (New York, 1949), pp. 63–84.
[88] *Ibid.*, pp. 74–75.
[89] *Ibid.*, p. 75.
[90] "The Hound", *Doctor Martino*, p. 55.
[91] *Ibid.*, p. 55.
[92] *Ibid.*, p. 70.
[93] *Ibid.*

Faulkner intends this, but he does define the antipathy which existed between the white man and the Negro as economic jealousy. The Negroes on the chain gang work the streets. Their crimes are not serious. The motive for putting them on the chain gang is perhaps to provide labor for the county at a cheap rate. Providing labor in this way prevents men like the murderer from having jobs. Perhaps this is the explanation that Faulkner wishes to give for the attitude of the white murderer. From this situation it is possible to establish a causal chain that moves back to the two evils. By contrast Faulkner makes the Negro convicts morally superior to the murderer. When the murderer begins to rationalize his capture, one of the Negroes tells him: "Hush up, white man. . . . Don't you be telling us no truck like that".[94]

In "The Fox Hunt" and "A Rose for Emily", the Negro contributes a verisimilitude of time and place and helps create tone and atmosphere. "The Fox Hunt" begins before dawn when three Negro stable boys, carrying lanterns, enter the stables and speak to the animals. After the Negroes enter the barn, a burst of "mellow and meaningless and idiotic" laughter floats out.[95] The Negro groom, however, is important for an understanding of the story.[96]

In "A Rose for Emily" the edict of Colonel John Sartoris that Negro women must not appear in public without aprons contributes to the reader's knowledge of Faulkner's use of "things" as symbols of quality and status. Emily Grierson's Negro servant was faithful to her while she lived and his last act, leaving her house after her death, is an act of consideration. Whatever knowledge he has of her disappears with him. In this way her memory is perhaps given some protection. In some respects he is one of Faulkner's faithful servants.

It is perhaps in this role of the faithful servant that Uncle Job in the story "Smoke" makes his contribution. His presence gives the story and the man who has been murdered a particular quality that can be visualized. The old man is a type. In his own inadequate way he felt that he had looked after the judge. For most of seventeen years he had sat all day in a passage outside the judge's office. In a sense his virtue is wholly in his intention, although he says "I looked after him like I promised Mistis I would".[97] The affection that he had for the judge and the loss that he feels after his death is expressed through his tears.

Many of Faulkner's stories may be said to be primarily concerned with the effect of the white man's sin upon the Negro. Essentially these stories show the effect of the idea of the Negro upon the white conscience of the South, postu-

[94] *Ibid.*
[95] "Fox Hunt", *Doctor Martino*, pp. 21–28.
[96] *Ibid.*, p. 30.
[97] "Smoke", *Knight's Gambit*, p. 31.

late the survival of the Negro, and accuse the South of moral wrong. As a group, the stories form a kind of polemic whose point of view is stated in the title *Go Down, Moses*.

The general characteristics of the Negroes in these stories are those pointed out in the discussion of Lucas Beauchamp. More specifically they are a simple, lowly, uneducated people. Although most of them are victims of circumstances that they cannot control, their insights into their situations are usually penetrating. As victims, these characters are usually morally superior to their oppressors. Many of them achieve victories through defeat. In most of the stories there is a chase motif in which the Negro character may use flight or evasion as a means of survival. The chase usually ends with the physical annihilation of the character, but it frequently is made to symbolize the character's moral victory. Sometimes the structure of the story, as for example that of "Pantaloon in Black" or "The Bear Hunt" or "Red Leaves", contributes to the development of character. If the revelation of character can be considered a different process from the development of character, it is preferable to say that Faulkner reveals character in these stories.

Violence contributes to these stories in several ways. In "Red Leaves", "That Evening Sun", "Go Down, Moses", "Dry September", "Pantaloon in Black", and "Mountain Victory" there is some form of what may be called the lynch or crucifixion symbol. In these stories this symbol, or motif, conveys an almost Christian meaning, and is the means of the Negro character's victory. In "Go Down, Moses" the reported act takes the form of legal justice. Faulkner does not show the act in any of the stories. Some of the stories are finished before Faulkner establishes the fact that acts of violence that resemble lynching or crucifixion will take place. In "Red Leaves", the violence is controlled and given the formal ritualism of tribal ceremony.

"In Centaur in Brass", "A Bear Hunt", "A Justice", "Was", the violence is mingled with a grotesque humor and does not result in the death of the Negro characters. The humor reveals the basic evil in the plot situations. There is a sense in which all of the stories in this group reveal their individual tragedies through comic methods. This may be called Faulkner's satiric method, a method that can be explained somewhat through the title of "Pantaloon in Black".

To interpret this title as meaning black trousers of a particular style does not contribute to the meaning of the story. However, if the term is defined in an historical sense, the title can be said to subsume the meanings of the story. According to the *New English Dictionary* the pantaloon was a character in Venetian comedy, represented as a foolish and vicious old man, who was the butt of the clown's jokes and his abettor in his pranks and tricks. It is supposed that the word pantaloon was derived from the name of San Pantaleone, who was at one time a favorite saint of the Venetians. Historically, the term has been applied in contempt to an enfeebled, tottering old man, a dotard, an old fool. Pantaleon, the name of a particular musical instrument invented by a German musician in the eighteenth century, may also suggest some of the meaning implicit in Faulkner's title. This instrument is a large dulcimer that has one or two hundred strings that are sounded by hammers held in the player's hands.

As Faulkner describes Rider, the central character in this story, he is stricken with grief by the death of his wife, and all of his actions are a result and an expression of that grief. The sheriff expresses the point of view of the white people who come in contact with Rider. His obvious failure to recognize Rider's grief, a central evidence of Rider's humanity, is a failure of sensibility. This failure shows that the sheriff and the white people of the town can only see Rider as the pantaloon. The events of the story represent a travesty on the ideal concept of human values. In this travesty, the clown or actor who initiates the grotesque or comic sequence is the white man. Rider is the pantaloon, the butt of his jokes. There is, of course, a sense in which life plays jokes on all men. The relation of pantaloon to sainthood is implicit in the story; for after his death Rider is a kind of saint. Rider may also be compared to a stringed instrument.

In the sense that Rider can be considered the butt of the white man's (the clown's) "jokes", so can all of the Negro characters in these stories be considered pantaloons acting out parts in a grotesque comedy.

"Pantaloon in Black" is the story of Rider, a young saw-mill worker, who when the story begins is beside the grave of the wife to whom he had been married for only six months. Rider's marriage marked for him the beginning of purposeful ordered living. For him it was a conscious affirmation, the placing of trust in one set of values and the rejection of another. His rejection of his past life is summed up in his statement "ah'm thu wid all dat".[98] When his wife dies after six months, Rider is grief-stricken, and for him life has lost its purpose. He not only grieves, but he tries to discover why his wife was taken from him. The story is not only of his effort to understand and master his grief, but it is of his effort to understand life. Just before the Birdsong boys come to kill him, he says: "Hit look lack ah just cant quit thinking".[99]

The first section of the story describes Rider's effort to organize the experience of death. This organization, for him, means a mastery of himself and a mastery of life. When he finishes the burial of his wife, he says that

[98] "Pantaloon in Black", *Go Down, Moses*, p. 138.
[99] *Ibid.*, p. 141.

he is going home. He rejects the offers of comfort and companionship that his aunt and his friends offer him. At home Rider's simple nature is revealed. It seems that he expects to see his wife's ghost, to talk with it, and perhaps to have the thing that has happened to him explained. For a moment he has the illusion (perhaps for him it was a real experience) of seeing her, but she fades and does not answer his questions. This is perhaps the beginning of his understanding that her death is final. He felt, during the moment that he sensed her presence, "between them that insuperable barrier of that very strength which could handle alone a log which would have taken any two other men to handle".[100] The events that follow this realization express Rider's grief and his effort to get away from his conscious futile effort to understand why his wife was taken from him.

In a way Rider's efforts are an attempt to escape from life. The escapes that he tries are not unusual. He attempts to escape through his work, through whiskey, and through gambling. In each one of these attempts, he tries to tax his body so greatly with a present experience that it will crowd out of his mind all thoughts of his wife. All of his efforts to do this are failures. He tells his aunt: "Nome, hit aint done me no good".[101] The intensity of his pain is probably expressed in his attitude toward her suggestion that he ask God for help. "Ef'n He God, Ah dont need to tole Him. Ef'n He God, He awready know hit. Awright, Hyar ah is. Leff Him come down hyer and do me some good".[102] When work and drink have failed as escapes, Rider tries gambling. Earlier in the evening he has told his uncle "Ah'm snakebit and pizen cant hawm me".[103] At this time this remark seems to have no particular meaning except that it is a phrase that men use when they drink or gamble. It is an appropriate phrase for Rider to use because, in a sense, work and drinking are games of chance. In the work Rider gambles his life. In drinking he risks his sobriety, which of course he wishes to lose. So far he has had a constant row of winnings. When he enters the toolroom of the saw-mill where the crap game is, he says: "Ah'm snakebit and bound to die".[104] This is a way of saying that he has the gambling fever, but the remark is also an accurate prediction of his death.

Rider's awareness of his own strength is affirmed in an odd way. Having suffered as he has from life, he feels that he is invincible. Even when he knows he is being cheated at craps, he can pass the dice and "let his money lay". But when another player follows his example, he exposes the dishonesty of the

[100] *Ibid.*, p. 150.
[101] *Ibid.*
[102] *Ibid.*
[103] *Ibid.*
[104] *Ibid.*

man who is running the game: "His left hand grasping the white man's wrist, his face still fixed in the rigid and deadened smiling, his voice equable, almost deferential. 'Ah kin pass even wid missouts [crooked dice]. But dese hyar yuther boys—' ".[105] This gesture is probably given some meaning through the title of the story. Rider is the pantaloon and the butt of the clown's whims. He accepts this place for himself. Ironically, he seems to defend it.

Rider's acceptance and defense of his role of pantaloon is an evidence that he is one of Faulkner's possessed characters. He is a man whose desperation continues to mount. His story contains aspects of the chase motif. In the first section of it he is fleeing from his own grief. In the second half, the chase that led to his death is described from the point of view of the sheriff. Throughout the story Rider is tormented, or chased, by the ideas in his mind.

Continually, he tries to free his mind of ideas through some external activity. The last scene in the prison reveals the intensity of this effort. The total effort of the portrait in the first section is to reveal Rider as a human being. The extent of Rider's possession and the pace and quality of the chase are revealed in the physical movement in the story.

Movement begins in the story at the graveside and increases in pace until Rider is seen in a frenzy of motion, through the sheriff's description, tossing the chain gang prisoners back and forth. "And Ketcham [a deputy] says that for a full minute that nigger [Rider] would grab them as they come in and fling them clean across the room like they was rag dolls".[106] Rider's movements are a means of establishing his character. He is a big person, "better than six feet and weighed better than two hundred pounds", and his movements are larger and stronger than those of the people around him.[107] They are not only larger but more intense, more precise; they show a greater skill and articulation of thought and act. Faulkner makes this clear in the first paragraph of the story. Throughout the story the pace and continuity of Rider's movement are emphasized. Sometime the movement is not Rider's but that of the things around him: "Then the dog left him".[108] "Then she was gone".[109] Usually sentences that indicate movement, as is true of the two above, come at the beginning of paragraphs and serve as indications of the new block of experience that Rider is to have. Many of the sentences begin with the adverb "then". Usually they are short sentences that give the block of experience that they introduce a quick, almost explosive beginning.

The explosive quality is an appropriate means of contributing to Rider's

[105] *Ibid.*, p. 153.
[106] *Ibid.*, p. 159.
[107] *Ibid.*, p. 135.
[108] *Ibid.*, p. 140.
[109] *Ibid.*, p. 141.

characterization, for he is a kind of superman. When he was a child, his aunt called him Spoot, but a knowledge of his adolescent physical and sexual superiority caused his friends to begin calling him by the more suitable name, Rider.[110] He can move almost as fast as a horse.[111] The timber "gang" that he heads moved almost twice as much timber between sunup and sundown as any other "gang" moved.[112] Rider handled, "at times out of the vanity of his own strength", logs which ordinarily two men would have handled.[113] His dog, part hound and part mastiff, is a big dog. He told his wife before her death: "Ah needs a big dawg. You's de onliest least thing whut ever kep up wid me one day, leff alone fo weeks".[114] Rider has more than physical strength. Even though his sorrow is deep, he controls his emotions and covers his wife's grave. At work the next day it is pointed out that he is "man-height again above the heads which carefully refrained from looking at him".[115] When he cried, his tears sounded like somebody dropping bird eggs.[116] In the afternoon, the day following his wife's funeral, he performed a feat that was more dangerous than any that he had done before. The action electrified the mill hands, and they watched him fearfully in silence, thinking that the log he handled alone would kill him. After this feat he buys a gallon of whiskey and drinks from it until it runs from his mouth, there being no more empty space inside his digestive tract. "Then drinking, he discovered suddenly that no more of the liquid was entering his mouth. Swallowing, it was no longer passing down his throat, his throat and mouth filled now with a solid and unmoving column which without reflex or revulsion sprang, columnar and intact and still retaining the mould of his gullet, outward glinting in the moonlight, splintering, vanishing into the myriad murmur of dewed grass".[117] The liquor does not make him drunk.

In each of his acts there is a perfection not found among lesser men. He cuts the throat of the night watchman who runs the dice game so "that not even the first jet of blood touched his hand or arm".[118] This perfect act comes at the end of the first section of the story and marks the climax of Rider's grief for his dead wife. His perfection is indicative of his isolation.

The quality and pace of the movement of the story not only characterize the chase motif and establish Rider as a possessed man, but they are the means

[110] *Ibid.*, p. 151.
[111] *Ibid.*, p. 142.
[112] *Ibid.*, p. 137.
[113] *Ibid.*
[114] *Ibid.*, p. 139.
[115] *Ibid.*, p. 144.
[116] *Ibid.*, p. 159.
[117] *Ibid.*, p. 149.
[118] *Ibid.*, p. 154.

of revealing his isolation. Rider is a man set apart. Other men cannot keep up with him. Paradoxically, his strength is also a weakness. The strength or weakness, however, makes Rider an individual rather than a social being.

Psychic distance is one of the chief means of establishing Rider's individuality. All of the people with whom he comes into contact are lesser beings than he. His aunt's husband is as tall as Rider; but he is a frail man, thin, almost weak. People generally, not only his aunt and her husband, are eager to do things for Rider, although many of them refrain from looking up at his face and eyes. Most people in the story recognize that he is different from them, fail to understand him, and, for these reasons, fear him.

A contrasting portrait of Rider is given by the sheriff in the second section of the story. The sheriff's failure is a failure of sensibility. His point of view is a result of the two evils. Of him it may be said "The fathers have eaten sour grapes".

"Them damn nigger," he said. "I swear to godfrey, it's a wonder we have so little trouble with them as we do. Because why? Because they aint human. They look like a man and they walk on their hind legs like a man, and they can talk and you can understand them and you think they are understanding you, at least now and then. But when it comes to the normal human feelings and sentiments of human beings, they might just as well be a damn herd of wild buffaloes." [119]

Rider is the individual used to prove this generalization. The sheriff repeats the details that the reader already knows and interprets them in terms of these observations: "His wife dies on him. All right. But does he grieve? He's the biggest and busiest man at the funeral".[120]

As Faulkner reveals the sheriff's failure of sensibility, he shows how the two evils operate. The superiority of the victim is made clear in several ways. The sheriff does not recognize human grief as it expresses itself in Rider. He expects Rider to try to escape after murdering the Birdsong, and he cannot understand his apparent disregard of danger. Rider's "Awright, white folks. Ah done it. Jest dont lock me up", he completely misunderstands.[121] He also fails to understand Rider's behavior while he is in jail. Faulkner gives a rather clear explanation of his behavior. He says, "Hit look lack Ah just cant quit thinking". The sheriff is puzzled by the expression, but he does not recognize it as an explanation of Rider's behavior.

As it is possible to say when speaking of the deputy, "the fathers have eaten sour grapes", it is also possible to say, "Father forgive them". Faulkner's use of the sheriff's reactions gives to Rider's lynching the paradoxical values of the crucifixion.

[119] *Ibid.*
[120] *Ibid.*
[121] *Ibid.*

In "Red Leaves", a Negro is again the superior victim whose death resembles the crucifixion. The story is divided into six sections. In the first of these, the treatment of the Negro is general. Doom (du homme), the chief of the tribe, is dead; and in accord with tribal custom his horse, his dog, and his body servant must be killed so that their spirits may accompany him on his journey into the other world. The plot of the story is developed through the effort of the tribe to capture the Negro man who had been Doom's body servant and the Negro's effort to save his life. The first three sections of the story are narrated from the point of view of an old and a young Indian who search for the Negro slave. In terms of their particular situation they state the evils that have come upon their region. At some time in the tribe's past the clan "gathered in squatted conclave over the Negro question".[122] They had no need for the slaves, but since slaves were too valuable to eat and had caused them so much trouble, they decided that they must do with them as white men did. They must "Raise more Negroes by clearing more land to make corn to feed them then sell them. We will clear the land and plant it with food and raise Negroes and sell them to the white men for money".[123] In part four of the story, the Negro who is the object of the search is the central character, and it is through him that the Negro's attitude toward life with the Indians is shown. As the first three sections are characterized by the Indians' preparations for the search, this section is characterized by the Negro's preparation for flight. In the last two sections of the story the Negro is captured and returned to the village for use in the death ceremony of the chief. In some respect this story resembles *Intruder in the Dust*; like Lucas, the Negro slaves have become tyrants over the minds and actions of their Indian owners.[124]

In section four a functional portrait of the Negro man is given and is used by Faulkner to integrate the thesis that makes up the general observations of the two Indians in the first three sections. The eventual destruction of the Indians and the survival of the Negro are implicit in the characterization of the Negro man. As a man the slave is created through an interrelation of his present with his past, through an interior monologue, and through the omniscient author. In the particular situation, the reader is made to understand the man's almost instinctive realization that he is going to die and finally, through the bite of a snake, that he does not wish to die. The reader is made aware of the man's fear through the sound of his breathing which grows louder and louder as he nears his death.

First, Faulkner describes the slave: "He was forty, a Guinea man. He had a flat nose, a close small head; the inside corners of his eyes showed red a little,

[122] William Faulkner, "Red Leaves", *These 13* (New York, 1931), p. 135.

[123] *Ibid.*, p. 136.

[124] *Ibid.* See also Kazin, p. 459. (His discussion of Faulkner's characterizations enables us to see how men get meaning from this world.)

and his prominent gums were a pale bluish and red above his square teeth".[125]
Then he is seen in one of the slave huts in the quarter. "In the dusk they
had faces like his, the different ages, the thoughts sealed inscrutable behind
faces like the death masks of apes".[126] But his fate is no longer the group fate.
He is singled out, a doomed man. "They looked at the body servant as he
stood before them, his eyeballs a little luminous. He was breathing slow and
deep. His chest was bare; he was sweating a little".[127] Breathing and sweating
set the body servant apart from the group. In one sense, he is already set
apart. He has been a body servant, and his task has been easier than those
of the other slaves. He has partaken of the same ease that his master has, and,
as that ease produced his master's death, so it must produce his. The quality
of his breathing announces the beginning growth of his fear. The growing fear
is paralleled with the beating drums that the slaves use in native fashion to
inform the doomed man of the progress of events in the community, and perhaps (Faulkner does not say) to guide him away from his pursuers.[128]

The drumming begins while the Negro hides in the barn waiting for his
master to die and to begin his flight. It is during this period of waiting that
the Negro's instinctive knowledge of his death becomes certain. Faulkner
explains this in terms of his consciousness splitting itself in two parts; one
part asking if he would live, and the other answering that he would die.[129]
The realization is not merely that he will die soon, but that "I am dead" as a
particular person who had a particular place in society. This realization
comes through a wish to indulge in a former social expression of life.

He imagined himself springing out of the bushes leaping among the drums on his barn,
lean, greasy invisible limbs. But he could not do that because man leaped past life, into
where death was; he dashed into death and did not die because when death took a man
it took him just this side of the end of living. It was when death overran him from behind
still in life.[130]

The image of himself barred from dancing, and a knowledge, through that
image, of the meaning of death, are consistent with the concept of the character. However, the statement of the meaning of the image must be taken
as Faulkner's effort to make explicit a sensibility that the slave felt, but because of its complexity could not explain.

The imagery in the Negro's mind changes when he becomes conscious of the
rats that run about below him in the stable. The Negro had eaten a rat when

[125] *Ibid.*, p. 147.
[126] *Ibid.*, p. 148.
[127] *Ibid.*
[128] *Ibid.*
[129] *Ibid.*, p. 150.
[130] *Ibid.*

he was a boy. For ninety days he had lived "in a three foot high 'tween deck" hearing "from topside the drunken New England captain intoning aloud from a book that he did not recognize for ten years afterward to be the Bible".[131] It was during that period that he had eaten the rat. "He had watched the rat, civilized by association with man reft of its inherent cunning of limb and eye; he had caught it without difficulty, with scarce a movement of his hand, and he ate it slowly, wondering how any of the rats had escaped so long".[132] The fate of the rat is identical with the fate of the Negro, and the meaning extends beyond him to include the fate of his Indian masters as well. Civilization has undone both of them.

At this point in the story there is a shift back to the present. The Negro watched all night the house in which has master lay dying. At dawn he saw the doctor leave and knew that Doom was dead. Then he watched the Indians begin preparations for the funeral. He noticed that the hound and the mare were brought and tied side by side. At sundown of that day he left the barn and began his flight.

With the beginning of the Negro's flight Faulkner emphasizes his isolation. He passed another Negro. The two men, the one motionless and the other running, looked for an instant at each other as though across an actual boundary between two different worlds.[133] During this encounter the Negro's breathing is again described to indicate his emotional state. "His broad nostrils [were] billowing steadily". He sees the two Indians who search for him on the second day of his flight. The two men are far away, and he decides to rest. The drums are still beating. That night he returns to the slave quarter. Again his isolation is emphasized through the action of the "head man" who gives him food and tells him that the dead may not consort with the living.

The pattern of pursuit emphasizes one of the moral themes of the story. The two Indians state this while they search for the Negro: "When have they [Negro slaves] ever been anything but a trial and a care to us?"[134] Symbolically, the Negroes' survival is affirmed when the Negro body servant meets an Indian on a log: "the Negro gaunt, lean, hard, tireless and desperate; the Indian thick, soft-looking, the apparent embodiment of the ultimate and supreme reluctance and inertia".[135] By contrast the Negro is given qualities of strength and action that make for survival. Following this affirmation of strength there is another: the ants which the Negro ate.[136]

---

[131] *Ibid.*
[132] *Ibid.*
[133] *Ibid.*, p. 152.
[134] *Ibid.*, p. 155.
[135] *Ibid.*, p. 156.
[136] *Ibid.*, pp. 156–157.

It is after he has eaten the ants that the Negro is struck three times by the cottonmouth moccasin. It is as if his flight from the Indians was merely an abstraction to which his intelligence had not given meaning; for he does not realize that he does not wish to die until the poison bite of the snake has given him an immediate fear of death. With the realization that he does not wish to die, although he knows that he must, the fourth section of the story ends.

Sections five and six contrast the strength of the Negro and the weakness of the Indians. The searchers are now led by Moketubbe, who, since Doom's death, is The Man and who is described as a "supine obese shape just barely alive, carried through the swamp and briers by swinging relays of men who bore steadily all day long the crime and its object, on the business of the slain [Moketubbe had poisoned his father]".[137] It should be pointed out that Moketubbe is twenty-six and already dropsical and near death, while the slave, at forty, is in perfect physical health, strong enough to throw off the effects of the snake bite. The reason for Moketubbe's weakness is clear. The egotism of Moketubbe's nature has developed in him a lust for the power (control and property) that was symbolized in the office of The Man, his father. Since the time when he was a child, this lust had motivated his actions. The tribal symbol of office is a pair of high-heeled red patent-leather shoes that The Man had brought back from France. Moketubbe has shown all of his life a desire to overthrow his father by stealing and playing with the shoes. As the Chief, and during the chase, Moketubbe may (in fact, should) wear the shoes. His feet, however, are too large for them; and wearing them, although he is carried in a litter, is so painful that he faints during the chase.[138] Thus, it is the pursuer who faints and not the pursued.

The slave allows himself to be taken, gives up the flight. At one time he was surrounded by Indians, but it is learned from their conversation that they were powerless to take him against his will: "But you turned him back?" "He turned back. We feared for a moment".[139] The fear that is admitted by the Indians by contrast is an indication of the strength of the slave. The slave has fear also, but his is of a different kind. After he discovers through the snake's bite that he wants to live, he is afraid of dying. The slave gives up flight, not because he has fear of the Indians, but as an acceptance of the inevitable. The acceptance is also a kind of self-mastery that is apparent in the slave when the Indians take him. "They could see him, naked and mud-caked sitting on a log, singing. They squatted silently a short distance away until he finished. He was chanting something in his own language, his face lifted to the rising sun. His voice was clear, full, with a quality wild and

137 *Ibid.*, p. 158.
138 *Ibid.*, p. 160.
139 *Ibid.*, p. 161.

sad".[140] The Indians acknowledge the superior quality of the Negro when they take him. "You ran well. Do not be ashamed".[141] This is the end of the fifth section of the story.

In the final section, Faulkner continues to contrast Indians and the slave. The ease of living like white men has made the Indians flabby and physically unremarkable:

The Negro was the tallest there, his high, close, mud-caked head looming above them all. He was breathing hard, as though the desperate effort of the six suspended and desperate days [his flight or evasion had lasted six days] had capitulated upon him at once; although they walked slowly, his naked scarred chest rose and fell above the close-clutched left arm [the snake bit him on that arm]. He looked this way and that continuously, as if he were not seeing, as though sight never quite caught up with looking.[142]

The contrasts in the scene are sharp. The Indians who mourn Doom are dressed "in their bright, stiff, harsh finery; the women, the children, the old men". The Negro is naked except for caked mud put on his body for protection against mosquitoes. Symbolically he represents the purity of the natural man contrasted to the decay that the Indians represent in their submission to their lusts. The contrasts in the scene resemble those that produce the tensions in El Greco's "St. Martin and the Beggar".

He is offered food that he cannot eat, and he asks for water that he cannot drink. His inability to eat and drink, the failure of his physiological functions to obey his will, indicates the conflict within the man who, at the beginning of the story's fourth section, says "I am dead" before he has begun to try to save his life, and who discovers that he wants to live only after he is bitten by a deadly snake. His effort to drink water gives this conflict meaningful expression:

They watched his throat working and the unswallowed water sheathing broken and myriad down his chin, channeling his caked chest. They waited, patient, grave, decorous, implacable; clansmen and guest and kin. Then the water ceased, though still the empty gourd tilted higher and higher, and still his black throat aped the vain motion of his frustrated swallowing. A piece of water-loosed mud carried away from his chest and broke at his muddy feet, and in the empty gourd they could hear his breath: ah-ah-ah.[143]

And so the last that the reader hears of the Negro is the sound of his breathing that has become audible and expressive of his fear of dying.

Thematically, "Dry September" is not different from "'Pantaloon in Black" and "Red Leaves". It is, however, primarily a study of attitudes toward the Negro rather than a study of Negro character. Will Mayes is guilty of no

[140] *Ibid.*, p. 162.
[141] *Ibid.*
[142] *Ibid.*, p. 163.
[143] *Ibid.*, p. 166.

crime. He is an innocent victim. His story shows how the two evils have conditioned thinking and acting in the South. Will is present in only one of the story's five sections. Faulkner does not describe his appearance. Will asks why the white men want him. They do not answer. "They worked busily about the Negro as though he were a post, quiet, intent, getting in one another's way. He submitted to the handcuffs, looking swiftly and constantly from dim face to dim face".[144] Will is passive and submissive until the men begin to strike him. Then "he whirled and cursed them, and swept his manacled hands across their faces and slashed the barber [who had defended him] upon the mouth".[145] Inside the car Will sat between the barber and the soldier with his limbs drawn close so that they did not touch the white men. Just before the barber, who refuses to participate in the lynching, leaves the car, Will speaks his name. He does not speak again and Faulkner does not call the reader's attention to him in any other way.

In this story, Faulkner's method is that of understatement. Will Mayes, like Lucas in *Intruder in the Dust*, is any Negro man. Like Hawthorne, and his attitude toward Hester's sin, Faulkner is more interested in examining the causes and results of lynching than he is in the crime itself. For this reason he does not give the details of Will Mayes' death.

The first paragraph of the story establishes its tone and mood:

Through the bloody September twilight, aftermath of sixty-two rainless days, it had gone like a fire in dry grass — the rumor, the story, whatever it was. Something about Miss Minnie Cooper and a Negro. Attacked, insulted, frightened: none of them gathered in the barber shop on that Saturday evening where the ceiling fan stirred, without freshening it, the vitiated air, sending back upon them in recurrent surges of stale pomade and lotion, their own stale breath and odors, knew exactly what had happened.[146]

The barber proves, although the other men in the room do not agree with him, that Will Mayes did not do whatever was done. One of the men in the shop asks, "Happen? What the hell difference does it make? Are you going to let the black sons get away with it until one really does it?"[147] Finally there is a reference to "our mothers and wives and sisters" and the men go out to lynch Will, in spite of the fact that the honor that they chose to defend had twelve years before "been relegated into adultery by public opinion".

The white men of particular communities lynch Rider and Will Mayes. Nancy of "That Evening Sun" may also be considered a lynch victim. Her husband murders her but he is merely the agent of the community. "That Evening Sun" is an exigent study of the terror felt by a Negro washer woman

144 "Dry September", *These 13*, p. 273.
145 *Ibid.*, p. 273.
146 *Ibid.*, p. 261.
147 *Ibid.*, p. 264.

who knows that her husband is going to kill her. The story is told by Quentin
Compson, years after it had happened. It is a childhood experience that
Quentin recalls. He recalls how Nancy looked with the bundle of clothes on
her head and her hat on top of the bundle. He remembers discovering that
whiskey was not responsible for Nancy's careless work habits. He remembers
that trouble Nancy had with Mr. Stovall.

Nancy is a victim of circumstances. She is a nigger. Perhaps she sought
white men. Faulkner does not say. He does describe her relation with Mr.
Stovall, the bank cashier, and a deacon in the Baptist church. Mr. Stovall
knocked her down and kicked her teeth out, but she kept saying, "It's been
three times now since he paid me a cent".[148] As a result of this public disturb-
ance, Nancy was put in jail. Like Rider's, Nancy's actions are misinterpreted.
The jailer tries to explain her attempted suicide and to destroy its significance.
"He said it was cocaine and not whiskey [it was neither], because no nigger
would try to commit suicide unless he was full of cocaine".[149]

Mr. Stovall represents the causal factor in Nancy's tragedy. It is perhaps
not possible to say that Nancy is better than he. In many respects she is not.
She, however, is honest. Mr. Stovall pretends to be what he is not. His attack
on Nancy on a Jefferson street was a pretense in defense of his reputation.
Nancy's arrest by the agent of the law was a further pretense toward the defense of that reputation. Even Mr. Compson defends Stovall when he tells
Nancy, "There's nothing for you to be afraid of now. And if you'd just let
white men alone". Selfishness is responsible for Nancy's plight. Mrs. Compson's attitude toward her represents this selfishness. She asks her husband,
"You'll leaves these children unprotected with that Negro about?"[150]

The title of the story is perhaps suggested by a phrase from the lyrics of
the "St. Louis Blues". Nancy, however, does not lament because her husband,
Jesus, has left her. She laments because she knows he will return. The woman
in the lyrics loves her man and we may suppose that Nancy loves Jesus. She
says that whenever he had two dollars, one was hers.[151] When it is suggested
that he may have taken another woman in Memphis, she says, "If he has, I
better not find out about it".[152]

We are told much less about Jesus than we are about Nancy. The Compson
children have been warned by their father to have nothing to do with him.
At times the woman who is said to be his mother will not say that he is her
son. "He was a short black man, with a razor scar down his face".[153] He is

[148] "That Evening Sun", *These 13*, pp. 235-242.
[149] *Ibid.*, p. 235.
[150] *Ibid.*, p. 240.
[151] *Ibid.*, p. 239.
[152] *Ibid.*
[153] *Ibid.*, p. 233.

shown to the reader briefly in the Compson kitchen where he has eaten his breakfast. The Compson children have noticed that Nancy's stomach is swollen. Jesus tells them that it is a watermelon. "It never come off of your vine, though", Nancy said.[154] Jesus says he can cut down the vine "it did come off".[155] Perhaps he can but he does not. Understandably, he must attack Nancy. Although Jesus is powerless to correct or rid himself of the evil in his life, he has a clear insight into its nature. In this respect he is like many of Faulkner's defenseless characters: " 'I can't hang around white man's kitchen', Jesus said 'But white men can hang around mine. White man can come in my house, but I cant stop him. When white man want to come in my house, I aint got no house. I cant stop him, but he cant kick me outen it. He cant do that".[156]

It is after Jesus leaves that Nancy's fear becomes specific. These fears and Nancy's character are made clear to the reader through small details of her behavior that the Compson children notice. Dilsey gives her a cup of coffee; and she discovers, like Doom's servant, that she cannot swallow. She drops her coffee cup, but she holds her hands stiffly curved as if the cup was still there. She looks at things without seeing them. The Compson children say she looks and talks as if she had emptied her eyes and voice. She tells the Compson children a story about a queen, but the experiences are her own. Although her hands are burned by a hot lamp chimney, she does not take them away until the children tell her to. She cries without knowing that she cries, and she makes at intervals a noise "not singing not unsinging".

The self-interest of the children is also made a means of revealing the fear that torments Nancy. Nancy is safe when the children are with her, so she makes excuses to remain near them. She seems to be aware that all of her efforts to keep them near her merely postpone her death, and her fear mounts as her efforts to remain near the children fail. Dilsey's illness gives her a brief respite because it is possible for her to stay in the Compson home for a few days. When Dilsey is well again, she must go back to her cabin at night. Her pathetic effort to persuade the Compson children to accompany her reveals her fear.

Once the children have been persuaded to follow her to the cabin at night, she must struggle to keep them there. Her stories fail to charm them. The popcorn burns, and she has no candy. When Mr. Compson comes at night to take them home, as she has feared he would, she decides to give up the struggle. Her fear had not become active until Jesus left her. When she receives word that he is back, although she has not seen him, she knows that he is going to

[154] *Ibid.*, p. 236.
[155] *Ibid.*
[156] *Ibid.*

kill her. When he leaves a recognizable sign in her room, she knows that nothing can save her. She is conscious that all of her efforts serve only to postpone the event. She says, "I can feel him. I can feel him now in this lane. He is hearing every word, hid somewhere waiting".[157] At the end of the story she says, "I reckon what I am going to get aint no more than mine". This acceptance of suffering makes her one of Faulkner's good people. When the Compsons leave her, she does not get up to bar her door. They see the light of her fire and hear her making the sound that was not singing as they go away.

In three of the Faulkner stories, "Was", "A Bear Hunt", and "Centaur in Brass", stories in which a chase is a central event, Faulkner uses a grotesque satire to develop his Negro characters. Each of these stories has some of the features of a detective story, although no one of them follows a formal detective story pattern. There is a chase in each of the stories, and evasion as a technique of survival is used by the Negro characters in each of them. In "Was" Uncle Buck and Uncle Buddy have trouble keeping their half-brother, Tomey's Turl, on the McCaslin plantation. At intervals he runs away to the Beauchamp plantation to court Tennie. When this happens, Uncle Buck goes to get him. The chase that always follows resembles a fox-hunt. Dogs are used, the scent is found and lost, and finally Tomey's Turl escapes capture. Uncle Buck and Mr. Beauchamp decide that they are tired of these periodic hunts, and so they play a game of poker to decide who will own both Turl and Tennie. Uncle Buck wins, and the story ends as he returns home with two slaves instead of one.

In "A Bear Hunt", a fun-loving white man plays a crude joke on a Negro man at a church picnic. Twenty years later the Negro man repays the joke. In "Centaur in Brass", Flem Snopes, who is a plant manager, steals brass fixtures and persuades, almost forces, a Negro employee, Tom-Tom, to hide the stolen brass in his barn. When a sufficient quantity of brass to be sold has been accumulated, Flem tells Turl, a Negro who works on the undesirable night shift in the plant, that he thinks Tom-Tom has been stealing brass and that he will give him Tom-Tom's more desirable job if he will go out to his home and find the brass. Instead of searching for brass, Turl begins a relationship with Tom-Tom's wife. There is a comic chase, and the offender is caught. The two men exchange the facts that they know about Flem Snopes and decide that Flem has been responsible for the adultery and that he plans to do them both harm. Following a plan of their own, they take the brass and hide it in the city water tank.

In each of these stories, white men treat Negroes with less respect than human beings are entitled to. In the first two stories, there is no intention to harm the Negroes. Uncle Buck does not enjoy chasing Tomey's Turl. The system of which he is a part demands the action of him. The harm done in the first two stories results from the evil inherent in the South's bi-racial living patterns. The case of Flem Snopes is different. His intention is to exploit the city that employs him as water superintendent, and to make the Negroes bear the blame for his dishonesty.

In "Centaur in Brass", the use of evasion as a technique for survival is illustrated. The Negro characters, Tom-Tom and Turl, do not at any point in the story disobey completely the directions of Flem Snopes. They evade them. Deliberate disobedience would be detrimental to their interests, but evasion, as they use it, is a means of convicting Flem Snopes of theft.

This story, essentially a comedy of manners and mores, is narrated by Harker, who is a white man. We can assume that Harker realizes that the story tells of the defeat of another white man by a Negro. The man who is defeated, however, is so despicable and has behaved so stupidly that Harker does not feel that he violates any convention by telling it. To the extent that it is a "Negro" story, it is the kind of story that a white man might tell white men. Frequently the Negro subject, as Turl is, may be present during the narration and may be jovially included in the comedy by proper chance remarks. A part of the story's irony is that Harker is only aware of its particular meaning. Its general meaning must escape him. For essentially, through the story's full meaning, Harker is narrating an example of the Negro's moral superiority.

The title of the story contributes to an understanding of its meaning in a special way. Flem Snopes and Major Hoxey, the town mayor, as a result of Mrs. Snopes's adultery with Hoxey, are united in an unnatural friendship. As a result of this friendship, Snopes becomes superintendent of the municipal water plant. Like a centaur, friendship between a Hoxey and Snopes is an unnatural, hybrid creation. It is a union of natures as diverse as are the natures of a man and a horse. The friendship between Tom-Tom and Turl is of the same kind. Turl seduces Tom-Tom's wife, and after Tom-Tom discovers the adultery, the two men, whose natures and personalities are diverse, become friends. The results of their friendship show that evil may be checked if not overcome. The Snopes-Hoxey friendship is made to promote evil and is based upon a perverse sense of moral value. The monument that Snopes makes for himself is also unnatural. When Turl and Tom-Tom move the brass from Tom-Tom's barn, they put it in the city water tank. The water becomes unfit for human use, but the city does not destroy the tank. Divorced from its function, the water tank has become a monument to Snopes's greed.

This story is divided into six sections. In the first of these, Flem Snopes is introduced, and the general outline of his character is developed. Selfishness, or greed, is the motivating principle of his character. The plot of the story is suggested in these sentences: "And so we believed that whatever his wife was, she was not fooling him. It was another woman who did that: A Negro woman, the new young wife of Tom-Tom, the day fireman in the power plant".[158] Then there is a paragraph that identifies Tom-Tom and describes him: "Tom-Tom was black: a big bull of a man weighing two hundred pounds and sixty years old and looking about forty. He had been married about a year to his third wife, a young woman whom he kept with the strictness of a Turk in a cabin two miles from town and from the power plant where he spent twelve hours a day with a shovel and bar".[159] The paragraphs that follow begin the action of the story. Tom-Tom has just finished cleaning the fires and is sitting smoking his pipe. Flem Snopes asks him how much the brass whistles weigh. Tom-Tom tells him ten pounds. Flem asks if it is solid brass, and Tom-Tom answers "If it ain't, I aint never seed no brass what *is* solid".[160]

Turl is introduced by Harker, the night engineer, as "that damn black night fireman that couldn't even read a clock face". Harker discovered Turl throwing coal into boilers from which the brass safety valves were missing. When Harker asks where the safety valves are, Turl tells him that Flem removed them. In the next paragraph, Faulkner explains the effect of Flem's theft, and his explanation serves to indicate the compatible nature of the work relationship between Harker and Turl. The reader's attention is then shifted to Tom-Tom, who watches Flem try with a magnet "a miscellaneous pile of metal junk". When the brass is separated from the other metals, Flem tells Tom-Tom to take it to his office. After Tom-Tom has done this, Flem asks how Turl and he get along. Before Tom-Tom answers, Harker, who is the narrator, compares Tom-Tom and Turl. Earlier Harker has called Turl that "damn black night fireman". The reader now learns that "black" was intended to designate Turl's race and not his color, for Harker tells us that "he was saddle colored where Tom-Tom was black". "I tends to my business", Tom-Tom said. "What Turl does with hisn ain no trouble of mine".[161] During the conversation Tom-Tom looks at Snopes as steadily as Snopes looks at him. Snopes tells Tom-Tom that Turl wants his job firing on the day shift. "So I want you to take this stuff out to your house and hide it where Turl can't find it and as soon as I get enough evidence on Turl I am going to fire him".[162]

[158] "Centaur in Brass", *Collected Stories*, p. 152.
[159] *Ibid.*, p. 152.
[160] *Ibid.*
[161] *Ibid.*, p. 155.
[162] *Ibid.*

Tom-Tom says that he knows a better way to prevent Turl from trying to get his job. Snopes says that this plan will get both Turl and Tom-Tom in jail. At the end of the discussion, in effect, Snopes tells Tom-Tom that he must take the metal home and hide it if he wants to keep his job. "And he kept his own counsel too. Because he had been firing those boilers for forty years, ever since he was a man. At that time there was but one boiler and he got twelve dollars a month for firing it, but now there were three and he got sixty and he owned his little cabin and a little piece of corn, and a mule and a wagon in which he rode into town and to church twice each Sunday, with his new young wife beside him and a gold watch and chain".[163]

At the beginning of section three, Snopes repeats with Turl the scene that he has been through with Tom-Tom in section two. He begins "What's this about you and Tom-Tom"? Where Tom-Tom is mature and dignified, Turl is young and carefree; but he is respectful toward Tom-Tom. This is apparent in his speech. Snopes tells Turl that Tom-Tom thinks he wants his day shift. Then he tells him how for two years Tom-Tom has been stealing brass in order to "lay it on" Turl and get him fired, "how only that day Tom-Tom had told him that Turl was the thief". He then tells Turl to go out to Tom-Tom's house and get the brass and bring it to him. He promises to put it "away somewhere" to use as evidence against Tom-Tom. Turl agrees to steal the brass from Tom-Tom for the same reason that Tom-Tom had agreed to take it home. He wants to keep his job. After Turl's agreement Harker gives the reader more information about him that serves to establish his character. He is a contrast to Tom-Tom. His reputation with women is known throughout the town.

Harker's characterization of Turl as a rather earthy Don Juan hints early in the story that it was Tom-Tom's wife who fooled Flem Snopes. "When I found out how he [Flem] had picked out Turl out of all the niggers in Jefferson that's prowled at least once (or tried to) every gal within ten miles of town to go out to Tom-Tom's house".[164]

Faulkner uses a surprise element at the beginning of section four. Turl creeps upon Tom-Tom's back porch and stoops over a figure on a cot and says, "Honeybunch papa's done arrived". Tom-Tom was on the cot disguised in one of his wife's gowns and holding a butcher knife by his side. Harker explains Tom-Tom's accidental discovery of his wife's infidelity. He had been given a "last year's watermelon which the local butcher had kept all winter in cold storage and which he had given to Tom-Tom, being afraid to eat it".[165] The melon made Tom-Tom's wife violently ill; and while she was in pain and fear of death, she confessed her sin with Turl. The next day Tom-Tom

[163] *Ibid.*, p. 156.
[164] *Ibid.*, p. 160.
[165] *Ibid.*

cooked breakfast and lunch for himself and for his wife. As she remained in bed all day, he fed her. When Turl crept upon his porch and touched him, he was waiting for him.

The events that follow are grotesquely comic. Turl turns to flee, and Tom-Tom leaps astride his neck and shoulders. His weight sends Turl off the porch "already running when his feet touched earth". The emphasis that Faulkner has given to the difference in the weight of the two men (Tom-Tom is at least fifty pounds heavier than Turl) is effective as a means of establishing in the reader's mind the ludicrous appearance of the "two of them a strange and furious beast with two heads and a single pair of legs like an inverted Centaur speeding phantom-like just ahead of the board-like streaming of Tom-Tom's shirt and just beneath the silver glint of the lifted knife, through the moony April woods". The comic value of this chase has some of the qualities of a Chaplin movie. Its pattern frustrates what is usually expected in a chase. When the pair are in the woods, Turl tries to rake Tom-Tom off his back by bumping into trees; "But he helt on so tight with one arm that whenever I busted him into a tree, I had to bust into the tree too".[166] The chase takes an unexpected turn when Tom-Tom begins squalling to be let down. They are approaching a ditch, and Turl has not seen it. Tom-Tom "grabbed my head with both hands and begun to haul it around like I was a runaway bareback mule and then I seed the ditch. It was about forty foot deep and it looked a solid mile across, but it was too late then. My feets never even slowed up. They run far as from here to that door yonder out into nekkid air before us even begun to fall. And they was still clawing that moonlight when me and Tom-Tom hit the bottom".[167]

Harker reports this incident as Turl told it to him. His narration gives to it most of the values found in black-face comedy skits, or in the perhaps unkind caricatures of Octavus Roy Cohen's Florian Slapey stories. Faulkner has been careful, however, in his selection of details and incidents. He has put them in such a context that it is not the incidents alone that reveal the character of the Negroes, but the whole moral framework and point of view that suggest the evil of Snopes's greed.

The materials of the comic element in the story come from the body of details found in comic stereotypes of Negroes. There are razors, whiskey, watermelon, confessions induced by fear of death, unfaithful wives, butcher knives, a man whose sexual proclivities are unusually great, and the idea that Negro women are unchaste. Harker says that Turl has "prowled" at least once every "gal" within ten miles of town. His modification "or tried to" is a parenthetical afterthought.

[166] *Ibid.*
[167] *Ibid.*, p. 164.

The story reveals, through its irony, a kind of etiquette of race relations. White men may say a number of things to Negroes about their marital and extra-marital relationships in a joking and friendly manner. This is supposed to indicate goodwill and kindly interest.[168] The Negro is supposed to accept these comments with a smile, but it is taboo that he make similar comments about the marital relationships of white men. Harker tells, in Turl's presence, about Tom-Tom's discovery of his wife's infidelity, and this to him seems a huge joke on Flem Snopes. Turl's reactions are not given, but it may be supposed that he smiles and accepts Harker's attention to him as a courtesy. Essentially, it is this etiquette of race relations, applied in a different area, that causes Snopes to suppose that he can steal the power company's brass with the aid of unsuspecting Negroes. Harker says at one point in the story: "Mr. Snopes [when Harker mentions a white man to a Negro he follows the convention of adding a title] is going to tell Tom-Tom how there is a strange tom-cat on his back fence. And whenever a nigger husband in Jefferson hears that, he finds out where Turl is at before he even sharpens his razor: Aint that so, Turl"?[169] Just as Harker presumes certain things about Turl's sexual morality, it is supposed that Negroes steal. The etiquette of race relations and the stereotypes are mutually dependent. Snopes attempts to use the etiquette and the stereotypes to his advantage.

The title of the story assists the reader in understanding what takes place between Tom-Tom and Turl after the plunge to the bottom of the ditch. Faulkner has already called the reader's attention to the physical image of the centaur. The friendship of the two men that begins in the ditch is a logical extention of the meaning of centaur. Before this incident, Faulkner has taken care to show that the two men are opposites and that they are not friends. Judged by conventional standards of behavior, friendship between them should not be possible. Tom-Tom, contrary to expectations, does not punish Turl:

He and Turl just sat there in the ditch and talked. Because there is a sanctuary beyond despair for any beast which has dared all, which even its mortal enemy respects. Or maybe it was just nigger nature. Anyway, it was perfectly plain to both of them as they sat there, perhaps panting a little while they talked, that Tom-Tom's home had been outraged, not by Turl, but by Snopes; that Turl's life and limbs had been endangered, not by Tom-Tom, but by Flem Snopes.[170]

The last sentence of this quotation explains why Tom-Tom did not punish Turl and contains the central meaning of the story. Tom-Tom and Turl did

[168] Bertram Wilbur Doyle, *The Etiquette of Race Relations in the South* (Chicago, 1937), pp. 12–17, 160–172.

[169] "Centaur in Brass", p. 162.

[170] *Ibid.*, p. 170.

as they did because of the white man. Flem Snopes is a personification of the two evils. Tom-Tom and Turl realize that they have been touched and forced to act by evil. The attitude toward Negro vices and patterns of behavior expressed here is essentially a restatement of the attitude expressed in "The Bear".

The passage also shows why Faulkner's use of situations may not be taken at its face value. Although Harker, who is telling this story, is a particular man representing a particular race and tradition, the story is not told entirely from his point of view. The omniscient author often interrupts his narrator's point of view and expresses his own. In the above quotation, Harker says, for example; "Because there is a sanctuary beyond despair for any beast which has dared all, which even its mortal enemy respects. Or maybe it was just nigger nature". Harker, the individual representing a particular race and tradition, is not likely to have possessed the insight represented in both of these sentences. The first sentence causes us to interpret the relation between Tom-Tom and Turl as Faulkner wants it to be interpreted. Tom-Tom and Turl observe a moral nicety that Harker, like the sheriff in "Pantaloon in Black", was likely to misunderstand and likely to accept as "nigger nature". The two sentences, however, should go together; for in the first Faulkner calls attention to a kind of natural morality as it operates in the world of nature. Without the second sentence it is possible to assume that he is calling Tom-Tom and Turl beasts. The second sentence prevents this by showing that even Harker does not think of "niggers" as beasts.

The fourth section of the story unfolds itself on a grotesquely comic level, a level that is kept from being slapstick by Faulkner's rhetoric and lyrical qualities that he gives the scenes through the intensity of the movement. The rhetoric, lyricism, description, and movement (elements that are not to be separated in their effect) create out of the materials of grotesque comedy something that resembles the fairy tale. As the story develops from the beginning of the centaur-like friendship, the grotesque elements of the comedy are submerged under a rather ironic dispensation of justice and morality. The framework is still comic, but within this framework Tom-Tom and Turl plan a just retribution for Flem Snopes. When Flem took the first three steam gauges from the boilers, he lied and said that he had used them as weights to control the flow of water from the city tank. Tom-Tom and Turl decide to take the brass from Tom-Tom's barn and put it in the water tank.

In section five, the action shifts to the power plant and Snopes discovers that he has been foiled. He asks Turl if he found the brass, and Turl tells him that Tom-Tom says there is no brass in his barn. When Tom-Tom is asked where the brass is, he tells Snopes that it is where he wanted it, "when you took them whistle valves off the boilers". Flem is in an awkward position. He cannot fire Tom-Tom and Turl. When the city auditor discovers the brass is missing, and Buck Connor, the city marshal, comes with a warrant to arrest Tom-Tom and Turl, Snopes, who has been outwitted in his own scheme, pays for the brass and a few days later he resigns from the power plant.

In the end, Tom-Tom and Turl are the victors. Flem Snopes tried to use them to satisfy his greed. The story as a whole illustrates the twin evils and their effects. In order to satisfy his greed Flem Snopes permits, and condones, or perhaps aids his wife's adultery. Stimulated by greed, he attempted, also, to use Tom-Tom and Turl. The reader does not know what the effects of Flem's sin are on his wife. Some of its effects upon Tom-Tom and Turl are made clear.

The story "Go Down, Moses", which summarizes the meaning of the stories discussed in this section, is a moral allegory that accuses the white man in the South of guilt and neglect in his treatment of the Negro, and suggests by its example that he must bear the burden of his guilt. The allegory uses factual details and is clearly related to the contemporary world. The contemporary world that is described grew from a past that is represented in several point-of-view characters, Mollie, Miss Worsham, and Gavin Stevens. The title of the story, and Mollie's use of Biblical myth as an accusation of the South, creates the allegory and provides a way of interpreting it.

The story is didactic in intention, although its thesis is not given explicit statement. It means most of the things that are more explicitly stated in *Intruder in the Dust*. As an allegory the story resembles a sermon. The first section, the profile of Samuel Worsham Beauchamp, is a kind of *exemplum*. Section two is an analysis of the meaning of the *exemplum*: an exposition of a desirable Southern attitude toward the Negro that is made clear through processes of discovery and acceptance of responsibility.

"Go Down, Moses" is the story of Mollie Beauchamp's grandson, and it is also Mollie's story. Samuel Worsham Beauchamp was born on the McCaslin plantation and left by his parents for Mollie to raise. She was old, and rearing a child was too much for her. At best she could love him, and that was not enough. Time, race, and place were stronger than her love. In 1940, at twenty-six, Samuel was condemned to die in the electric chair. His life had been a succession of crimes, whose evidence could be seen in his face as he lay on his cot talking with a census taker. He was tired of life. Faulkner says his eyes had seen too much. Somehow his grandmother learned of his trouble. By 1940 she was very old and her mind weak; but when she heard, she walked the seventeen miles from the farm to town. The white people whom she visited and asked for help were kind and did not tell her what her grandson's crime and punishment had been. They told her he was dead; and because she wanted it, they brought his body home. The old woman insisted that the details of the funeral be "proper". The white people of the town paid the expenses — over two hundred dollars to bury a Negro they had cheated out of life.

The profile of Samuel Worsham Beauchamp, as he appeared to a census-taker in the Illinois prison just before his death, was cryptic:

The face was black, smooth, impenetrable; the eyes had seen too much. The negroid hair had been treated so that it covered the skull like a cap, in a single neat ridged sweep, with the appearance of having been lacquered, the part trimmed out with a razor, so that the head resembled a bronze head, imperishable and enduring. He wore one of those sports costumes called ensembles in the men's shop advertisements, shirts, and trousers matching and cut from the same fawn-colored flannel, and they had cost too much, with too many pleats; and he half lay on the steel cot in the steel cubicle just outside which an armed guard had stood for twenty hours now, smoking cigarettes and answering in a voice which was anything but a Southern voice or even a Negro voice the questions of the spectacled young white man sitting with a broad census-taker's portfolio on the steel stool opposite.[171]

The paragraph describes Samuel's appearance and his behavior. There is an artifice that Faulkner does not like in the hair, the ensemble, and the voice that was not Southern and not Negro. The "black, smooth, impenetrable" face was not human; did not reflect properly human experience. In explanation of this, Faulkner says "the eyes had seen too much". The man seen through the eyes of the census-taker is an alias. He is a man who has given up an identity that circumstances would not allow him to fulfill. The man that Samuel Worsham Beauchamp might have been would not have needed to leave Mississippi, would not have needed to murder a policeman in Illinois. The man who does kill is not Samuel. The murderer is a man whose occupation was getting rich too quick, a materialist who had fallen heir to, and used, the two evils to satisfy a frustrated egotism.[172] Samuel says, "It was another guy killed the cop", not the person he should have been.

That the eyes had seen too much can be judged from Samuel's blasé attitude; from the way he snapped the ash from his cigarette and said that it would not matter to him whether his body was taken home or not.[173] As Faulkner describes Samuel, he is a symbol characterized by three predicate adjectives, impenetrable, imperishable, enduring. At the end of the story, Faulkner calls Samuel the slain wolf.

The events that lead up to Samuel as he is first seen are sketched in through information that his grandmother and Gavin Stevens give the reader. During

[171] "Go Down, Moses", *Go Down, Moses*, p. 369.
[172] *Ibid.*, p. 369.
[173] *Ibid.*, p. 370.

the year that the boy had spent in Jefferson, he had been known as Butch Beauchamp. He was the son of Mollie's oldest daughter, "orphaned of his mother at birth and deserted by his father". Mollie had attempted to raise him, but at nineteen he had come to town, ordered by Roth Edmonds to leave his farm. In town he had been in and out of jail. He had been "caught red-handed whereupon he had struck with a piece of iron pipe at the officer who had surprised him and then lay on the ground where the officer had felled him with a pistol-butt, cursing through his broken mouth, his teeth fixed into something like furious laughter through the blood. Then two nights later he broke out of jail and was seen no more".[174]

His success in the city is summarized by Stevens in a brief paragraph: "He had a fair trial, a good lawyer — of that sort. He had money. He was in a business called numbers, that people like him make money in. . . . He is a murderer. He shot that policeman in the back. A bad son of a bad father. He admitted, confessed it afterward".[175] It is significant that Faulkner says "that people like him" rather than "Negroes like him", for in this way we are told that Samuel's failure is a human, not a Negro, failure. The facts that Stevens gives about Samuel are realistic. Most of them express a legalistic point of view. Stevens says some of "the papers of that business had passed over his desk".

Mollie does not know the factual details, but she does know instinctively that harm has come to her grandson. "Roth Edmonds sold my Benjamin. Sold him in Egypt. Pharoah got him. . . ." It is Mollie's knowledge that causes Gavin Stevens to look beyond the facts, beyond what was useful, legally, in evaluating Samuel. Mollie's knowledge enables him to see that when Samuel is "caught redhanded" his capture and its circumstances do not constitute an isolated fact. As Mollie says, the fact extends back to Roth Edmonds's order to Butch Beauchamp to leave the McCaslin plantation, and beyond that (for Gavin Stevens's logic is more precise than Mollie's) to the beginning of the two evils. Social forces and a particular heredity sold Samuel into Egypt. Stevens refers to Samuel as "a bad son of a bad father". The statement is true in two ways, but for the allegory the second meaning is more significant. Samuel's father begot and deserted him. At the time that Samuel was "caught red-handed", his father was already in the State Penitentiary for manslaughter. On the other hand, Samuel was sired by a particular society.

Mollie tells Stevens: "And you the Law. I wants to find my boy". When Stevens has found Samuel, not only in the sense of where he was, but also in the sense of who and what he was, Miss Worsham tells him that he must bring

[174] *Ibid.*, p. 372.
[175] *Ibid.*, p. 375.

his body home for proper burial. So far in the story, Stevens has recognized a situation without recognizing the part he had to play in it. Faulkner relates Miss Worsham to Mollie. Like her, she was quite old. In fact, it is about Mollie that she goes to see Stevens. At first, and superficially, Miss Worsham's concept of responsibility seems to be the same as that of the wife of Gabriel Pendleton in Miss Glasgow's novel *Virginia*. Miss Worsham asks, "Can nothing be done? Mollie's and Hamp's parents belonged to my grandfather. Mollie and I were born in the same month. We grew up as sisters". The parallel to *Virginia* is superficial because it is doubtful that Gabriel Pendleton could say that he grew up with a Negro as brothers grow up. Miss Worsham makes her plea to Gavin Stevens in response to Mollie's human need. She wants to protect Mollie from the knowledge of the manner of her grandson's death. "He is the only child of her oldest daughter, her own dead first child. He must come home", she says.[176] Miss Worsham not only recognizes that Samuel's body must be brought home; poor as she is, she gives the money that she thinks is sufficient to bring it home properly prepared for burial.

From the beginning of the second section of the story through Miss Worsham's visit to Stevens's office, Stevens is learning about the South's need. Her visit makes his responsibility clear to him. The arrangement of the details of Samuel's funeral in accord with the wishes of Mollie and Miss Worsham (traditional points of view applied to contemporary problems) shows his acceptance of that responsibility.

When Stevens visits Miss Worsham's home after arranging for the funeral, he finds it to be a house of mourning. Mollie's brother, Hamp Worsham, meets him at the door and tells him that Miss Worsham is up in "the chamber", the spare bedroom that Miss Worsham has provided in sympathetic hospitality for Mollie. Hamp adds, as he shows Stevens up the stairs, "We all dar". Hamp's "we" includes, in its broadest meaning, all of the people of the South. In the room the group is small, but formally ceremonial. They are seated, Mollie (not larger than a ten-year-old child), Miss Worsham, and Hamp's wife, "a tremendous light-colored woman". Mollie is in the only rocking chair in the room. Stevens and Hamp join the circle around the hearth, "the ancient symbol of human coherence and solidarity", on which a fire smouldered, although it was summer. Symbolically, through the ritual of the wake, the South had gathered to mourn the death that it had permitted if not caused.

The three Negroes in the room take part in an oral lament that begins after Stevens tells Mollie "He'll be home the day after tomorrow, Aunt Mollie".

---

[176] *Ibid.*, p. 376.

(Perhaps this is a statement of Faulkner's prophecy and belief that things are going to be better for Negroes in the South. In essence, the meaning parallels that in Isaac McCaslin's advice to the woman in "Delta Autumn"). Faulkner describes this as a strophe and antistrophe of the sister and brother accompanied by the wordless singing of Hamp's wife. " 'Sold my Benjamin', she said. 'Sold him in Egypt'. 'Sold him in Egypt', Worsham said. 'Roth Edmonds sold my Benjamin'. 'Sold him to Pharoah'. 'Sold him to Pharoah and now he dead' ".[177] Through the Biblical myth alluded to in the lament, the particular situation is given meaning, meaning that becomes clearer when Stevens apologizes to Miss Worsham for intruding.[178] Miss Worsham tells him "It's our grief", and includes him among the mourners.

The title of the story has a particular relation to the oral lament. The lament is a symbolic statement of fact; it is not a request. Earlier in the story, however, Mollie has told Stevens "You the Law". Near the end of the story Faulkner calls Stevens "The designated paladin of justice and truth and right". (Paladin, according to the *New English Dictionary*, derives a part of its meaning from the name and function of Count Palantine, most famous of the peers or warriors of Charlemagne's court, a renowned champion.) In the Biblical myth, Moses is the lawgiver who told Pharoah to let the children of Israel go. Moses is one of the children of Israel. He is not an outsider: Stevens's relation to Moses and to the South, especially after Miss Worsham tells him "It's our grief", is clear. It is in this way, and through Stevens's actions, that Faulkner makes the title functional in the story. The lament itself reminds the reader of the Negro spiritual, "Go Down, Moses", from which it is taken. The spiritual describes Moses's command from God to tell Pharoah to let his people go. It is the title, therefore, that gives the story its didactic meaning.

The funeral procession symbolized the possibility of the South's solving the Negro problem. Samuel Worsham Beauchamp's body was brought home from the "outside" and given a proper burial through the efforts of the people of his home. The people were "in formal component complement to the Negro murderer's catafalque: the slain wolf".[179] The cars were arranged in the procession in an order that may suggest the method that Faulkner felt should be followed in solving the South's problems. Stevens and the newspaper editor, the representatives of public opinion and the law, were joined in the first car behind the hearse. Miss Worsham and Mollie, who symbolized a human relationship not debased by particular factors of race and servitude and who

[177] *Ibid.*
[178] *Ibid.*, p. 381.
[179] *Ibid.*

each recognized evil, right, and responsibility, rode in the second car. There were more than a dozen cars, but these two led the rest.

The group of short stories that Faulkner calls *The Unvanquished* are closely related stories and may be considered a novel. Essentially, they are quite different from the Faulkner materials discussed so far. Irving Howe's suggestion about the relations between children in Faulkner accounts for this difference. The connotations of race only begin to apply when Bayard and Marengo cease to be boys and become adults. Bayard becomes aware of the change when he goes away to school. If the stories are treated as a unit, their total import is perhaps more tragic than that of some of the stories discussed already; for in them, two boys are forced to deny the existence of the first fifteen years of their lives in order to begin to live as adults in their world.

The stories reveal the Negro's tragedy in other ways, too, by showing the after-effects of slavery. Although the tone is pleasanter and the racial events less startling, the Negro is a victim in these stories, as he has been in the stories already discussed.

The events in *The Unvanquished* take place during the Civil War and shortly after its end. The principal Negro character is Marengo (Ringo), the boy companion of Bayard Sartoris, the child narrator. The boys are the same age and (as is mentioned in the discussion of Lucas) their friendship and their common interests usually submerged their knowledge of their difference of race.

Before the Sartoris home is burned, the conventions of living are constant reminders of the differing racial status of the two boys. The boys do not eat together, and Ringo must sleep on a pallet beside Bayard's bed. Except for differences of this kind, their activities, and frequently punishments for those activities, are interrelated and equal. In some of their ventures Bayard leads, but that is not a rule.

There is no difference in the method Faulkner uses to create Marengo from that used to create Bayard. The boys are individualized in terms of racial status, but not in terms of racial difference. Their separation and distinction comes only when they reach maturity and have to accept their individual roles in society. This individuation is social in nature and origin. The individual character is shaped by Faulkner to fit the social role that it must play in life.

The question of race and its relation to humanity is answered through a more or less constant comparison of Bayard and Marengo. Through this comparison Faulkner shows that the Negro boy is "smarter" than the white boy, that his intellectual aptitude is greater. The only difference that mattered to the boys was their difference in experience and knowledge of the world of the senses. This Faulkner illustrates through Marengo's request that Granny (Bayard's grandmother) read to them about "cokynut cake", which the war had deprived him of the possibility of tasting. Bayard is sure that he has eaten coconut cake, but Marengo is not certain that he has tasted it. He tries to make this uncertain knowledge certain by having Granny read to him about the cake from a cookbook.[180] There is a similar competitive intellectual curiosity expressed in Marengo's eagerness to see the railroad that Bayard has seen.[181]

The characters of the two boys are revealed through their actions and attitudes rather than through descriptions of their persons. To some extent this makes them representative rather than particular. When Faulkner does give physical details of his Negro characters, he usually makes these details serve some purpose in addition to identification and individuation. Marengo's uncle's head, for example, while Bayard and Marengo observe it during their play at reproducing the fall of Vicksburg, resembles a cannon ball. Perhaps it always does, but directing the reader's attention to the fact while the children play at war, not only describes a shape accurately, but reveals something of the intensity of the illusion that the children have created.

In each of the stories in *The Unvanquished* the reader is convinced that the reactions are boys' reactions. The treatment of the scene in which they attempt to shoot a Yankee soldier is characteristic of this. The sentiment they show toward the Mississippi dirt when they think they are leaving the state is another such incident. For them, in spite of their awareness of hardships and fear, Rosa Millard's wagon trek to search for her son-in-law's stolen silver and mules is a boy's paradise of new experiences. It is through his reactions to these experiences that the character of Ringo is established.

Perhaps the episodes that reveal most of Ringo's character are those in which he helps Mrs. Rosa Millard steal horses from the Yankees and then sell them back to them, and those in which he goes with Bayard to avenge her murder.

In the first of these episodes, Ringo shows the maturity that often develops in children as a result of necessity. The times made unusual demands, and Ringo helps Mrs. Millard in meeting those demands by helping her steal from, and resell to, the Yankees horses and mules. The manner in which Marengo meets this necessity is shown in this instance: "He had even learned to draw, who had declined even to try to learn to print his name when Loosh [his uncle] was teaching me [Bayard]; who had learned to draw immediately by merely taking up the pen, who had no affinity for it and never denied he had not but

[180] *The Unvanquished*, p. 56.
[181] *Ibid*.

who learned to draw simply because somebody had to".[182] Marengo's maturity of action is also matched by physical growth and his beginning to treat Bayard as if he were a child. "And he had got to treating me like Granny did — like he and Granny were the same age instead of him and me".[183] Marengo identifies himself with the Southern cause. He recognizes the quality of the people with whom he associates. This recognition does not allow him to trust Ab Snopes or to call him "Mister". When Mrs. Millard reminds him to say "Mister", he says "all right", an indication that he understands the etiquette she wishes him to observe, but he does not show Ab the courtesy that Mrs. Millard demands.

Marengo not only drew the map that showed the various counties and towns where Yankee troops were stationed and the nature of Bayard's and his transactions, the number of animals they had stolen from or sold to the troops, but he planned with Mrs. Millard their activities. While they worked at the disposal of the animals, he showed considerable poise and self-confidence. There is nothing of the self-effacement of the slave in him. When he waited for Mrs. Millard to make a decision:

Ringo didn't seem patient or impatient either; he just stood there, thin and taller than me [Bayard] against light from the window scratching himself. Then he began to dig with his right-hand little finger nail between his front teeth; he picked at his front teeth and spat something, and then he said, "Must been five minutes now." [Mrs. Millard had been trying to make a decision.] He turned his head a little toward me without moving. "Get the pen and ink", he said.[184]

The vulgar gestures that describe the boy reveal a lack of training in deportment which, no doubt, is a result of his being a slave. These same gestures reveal his poise and self-confidence.

At the church, when Mrs. Millard distributes the profits from her scheme among the needy of the community, Ringo must sit in the balcony, but segregation does not destroy his poise and confidence. Faulkner suggests this through a contrast. When Mrs. Millard walked into the church, the needy people would look at her exactly as Bayard's father's fox hounds would look at him when he would go into the dog run.[185] Marengo carries the book, a record of Mrs. Millard's charity to her neighbors, and Bayard sees, although they sit in different places, something of his worth and value because of this. "Ringo had the book; he went up to the gallery; I looked back and saw him leaning his arms on the book on the balustrade".[186] Ringo not only carries

[182] *Ibid.*, p. 142.
[183] *Ibid.*, p. 143.
[184] *Ibid.*, p. 144.
[185] *Ibid.*, p. 152.
[186] *Ibid.*, p. 153.

the book, but he keeps the accounts. "Ringo read the names off the book, and the dates, and the amount they had received before".[187] When the distribution of money was finished, Ringo closed the book and got the receipts together.

In many ways Ringo illustrates Faulkner's idea that the main question is what "quality" *does* rather than *is*. Ringo's attitude toward the South, a means that Faulkner employs to show his quality, is reflected in the things he does and says. Speech is an aspect of action. On one occasion Ringo has been drawing the plantation house as he remembers it before it was burned. He looks up from his work and sees a Yankee officer coming toward him. "Gre't God, ain't we gonter never get shet of them"? he asks.[188] The officer asks Ringo what his drawing is. Ringo answers that it is a house, but he does not interrupt his activity to look up at the officer. While he works, he adds, "Look at it". The officer looks from Ringo's drawing to the spot where the house had been. "You're drawing it like it used to be". " 'Co-rect', Ringo said. 'What I wanter draw hit like hit is now? I can walk down here ten times a day and look at hit like hit is now. I can even ride in that gate on a horse and do that' ".[189] The incident reveals the same love for the South and hatred of those who injured it that is found in the white characters. This loyalty to the South is further illustrated in Ringo's attitude toward Ab Snopes. Ringo realizes that Ab has told the Yankees of their dealing in horses and mules, that he has been a traitor to the South. This is his reason for not giving him the courtesy of a title. When Mrs. Millard is finally convinced of Ab's treachery, she does not remind Ringo of his lapse in conventional usage. Ringo not only realizes that Ab has been a traitor, but, like many of Faulkner's good characters, he recognizes the essential evil of a Snopes nature. He tells Mrs. Millard, "Do you reckon he was going to be satisfied until he sold them last nineteen mules to somebody"? The situation in which Ringo does call Ab "mister" is ironic. Ab is caught when running away from the punishment that he fears for having played an unconscious part in Mrs. Millard's death. Bayard has knocked Ab down in the road. Ringo picks him up and tries to force him to stand and face Bayard. It is then that he says, "Stand up, Mr. Ab Snopes".[190]

Faulkner does not spoil Ringo as a child by giving him strength and maturity that are essentially adult. His simplicity, directness, and lack of guile are essentially childlike. He makes a child's mistakes. The quality of his character is seen when he violates Mrs. Millard's taboo against swear-

[187] *Ibid.*, p. 381.
[188] *Ibid.*, p. 159.
[189] *Ibid.*, p. 160.
[190] *Ibid.*, p. 200.

ing and is sent to get soap to wash his mouth. Bayard, who has had this same punishment, watches him at the spring and hears him repeat the forbidden word when he is finished washing his mouth. "I still says we done damn well", he said.[191]

In the second episode that is of importance in revealing Ringo's character, the two boys set out to avenge the murder of the woman who has been Granny to both of them. During part of their mission, which in reality is too ambitious for children, they are accompanied by old Buck McCaslin. In this episode both of the boys behave very much as Faulkner's "possessed" characters do. They are convinced of the rightness of the activity they are engaged in. The knowledge of what they must do becomes a goad, an almost physical thing that drives them during all of their waking hours, and at night shapes their dreams. Bayard leads because Mrs. Millard was his blood relative, but Ringo helps him plan and helps him attack when the enemy is theirs. During the encounter with Grumby, the murderer, Bayard notices Ringo's participation: "I saw Ringo, in the air, looking exactly like a frog, even to the eyes, with his mouth open and his open pocket knife in his hand. . . . I saw Ringo straddle of Grumby's back and Grumby getting up from his hands and knees and I tried to raise the pistol only my arm wouldn't move. Then Grumby bucked Ringo off just like a steer would and whirled again, looking at us, crouched with his mouth open".[192]

A discussion of the characters in this group of related stories should include some mention of Loosh, Ringo's uncle, and of the Negroes who were "going to cross Jordan".

Loosh is a Negro who deserts the Sartoris plantation when the Yankees come to Jefferson. Faulkner does not give the details, but he allows the reader to suppose that Loosh has had secret meetings with the Yankees and that they have kept him informed of the progress of the war. This is made clear in "My Grandmother Millard", a narrative about the people and events in *The Unvanquished* in which the events in all of these stories take place after the Emancipation Proclamation has been made official.[193]

Loosh, or Lucius, knows that he is free. He talks to Bayard and Ringo about the battles that the South has lost, the fall of Vicksburg and Corinth, and says that soon the Yankees would have all of Mississippi and Yoknapatawpha County and that all of the "niggers" would be free.

Loosh represents the slave who is torn between two loyalties, a loyalty to himself and a loyalty to his former owners. He is a strong person in mind and

---

[191] *Ibid.*, p. 169.
[192] *Ibid.*, p. 210.
[193] "My Grandmother Millard", *Collected Stories*, pp. 667–700.

body, and his attitude toward life is aggressive. Loosh's position is essentially tragic because he has no preparation for his freedom; he has no place to go. This tragedy is made clear through the Negroes who are "going to Jordan". Loosh also explains a part of the fear of the Negro that grew in the slave owners. In these stories, Loosh is watched by Ringo and Bayard. His mother and his wife are afraid of what he may do. In "My Grandmother Millard", Louvinia, Loosh's mother, tells Mrs. Millard that Loosh plans to follow the Yankees to freedom.[194] It is Loosh who helped to bury the Sartoris silver, and it is he who shows the Yankees where it is buried. This latter act may be called one of courage and faith, however, rather than one of treachery — faith in the promise of freedom and courage to defy his former owners. Loosh is a tragic figure because he is foolhardy. He cannot know as Mrs. Millard does that he is leading his wife and himself into "misery and starvation".[195]

When Loosh is first seen in *The Unvanquished*, his eyes [are] a little red in the inner corners as Negroes eyes get when they have been drinking". Only Loosh has not been drinking. The reader later learns that the knowledge of coming freedom has had the same effect as whiskey upon him. Ringo and Bayard become suspicious of Loosh. They are playing war, and according to their knowledge Vicksburg has not fallen. But Loosh demolished the Vicksburg that they had built of chips with a sweep of his hands. When John Sartoris comes home, he confirms the truth of what Loosh has implied. Then suspicion of Loosh begins in earnest. This suspicion increases when it is discovered that Loosh rides away on some secret purpose after his work is done at night. Loosh rides in the direction of Corinth. When he returns, the two boys look in through his windows and learn what he has been doing. They hear Loosh's wife ask, "You mean they gwinter free us all?" and Loosh answers "Gen'ral Sherman gonter sweep the earth and the race gonter all be free!"[196] During the time that Loosh talks about freedom, he looks as if he is drunk; and he appears to be under a spell.

When the Yankees come, Loosh shows them the silver; and with a bandanna-wrapped bundle thrown across his shoulder and with his wife Philadelphia following him, he leaves the Sartoris plantation. Faulkner describes Loosh as not understanding what he was doing, moving as if he were in a dream. Loosh tells Mrs. Millard: "I going. I done been freed; God's own angel proclamated me free and gonter general me to Jordan. I don't belong to John Sartoris now; I belong's to me and God".[197] When he is asked about the

[194] *Ibid.*, pp. 670–671.
[195] *The Unvanquished*, p. 86.
[196] *Ibid.*, pp. 25–26.
[197] *Ibid.*, p. 85.

silver, he say: "Where John Sartoris? Whyn't he come and ax me that? Let God ax John Sartoris who the man that give me to him. Let the man that buried me in the black dark ax that of the man what dug me free".[198] Both of these passages are spoken when Loosh is in a trance-like condition. This unreal quality is used to characterize the hordes of Negroes from Mississippi and Alabama who followed the Yankees, "Going to cross Jordan" to their freedom. Loosh symbolizes the plight of these Negro men who were recently slaves.

Faulkner asserts that the evils of slavery were recognized by Southern planters before the Civil War and that war itself served to confuse and intensify these evils. In *The Unvanquished* he shows that the majority of the slaves had no idea what freedom was, that they had confused it in their minds with the coming of the Day of Judgment. The crossing of the river Jordan and entry into the land of Canaan, the land of pure delight, had become a vitalized symbol in their minds. When the Federal troops invaded the South, the freed slaves began a frenzied march to the river Jordan. Any river becomes Jordan, and they filled the roads and were drawn toward it by some inner necessity:

We couldn't count them; men and women carrying children who couldn't walk and carrying old men and women who should have been at home waiting to die. They were singing and walking along the road singing, not even looking to either side. The dust didn't even settle for two days, because all that night they still passed; we sat up listening to them, and the next morning every few yards along the road would be the old ones who couldn't keep up any more, sitting or lying down and even crawling along, calling to the others to help them; and the others—the young strong ones—not stopping, not even looking at them. I dont think they even heard or saw them. "Going to Jordan", they told me. "Going to cross Jordan".[199]

In *The Unvanquished*, the development of Negro character is dependent upon an omniscient narrator who sees his characters through the eyes of a child and from the point of view of a child. This provides that, in order to achieve verisimilitude, Faulkner does not use many of the formal devices that are found in the stories whose point-of-view character or narrator is an adult. In these stories Faulkner does not often analyze the minds of his characters. The rhetorical pattern is not as complete as that in many of the other Faulkner stories. The progression of the stories is more or less chronological. There is not an extensive use of paradox. The stories do indicate through the two boys a perfect knowledge of country ways. The speech of the characters contributes to the reality of time and place. There is in places a union of con-

[198] *Ibid.*
[199] *Ibid.*

crete historical details with lyricism, although the rhetorical flights are kept simple.

III

In the short stories above, Faulkner suggests, as he does in the title and content of "Go Down, Moses", that the South must assume a moral responsibility toward the Negro. This suggestion receives full development in his novels. There is also a full treatment in the novels of miscegenation and of the concept of the faithful servant.

Negro characters appear in most of Faulkner's novels. They are perhaps his major concern in *Intruder in the Dust, Go Down, Moses* (if this collection is a novel), and *Light in August.* Much of his attention is devoted to them in *Soldiers' Pay, Sartoris, The Unvanquished, Sanctuary, The Sound and the Fury, Absalom, Absalom!, Requiem for a Nun,* and *A Fable.* Although there are references to Negroes in most of Faulkner's novels, several of the novels are not discussed in this essay because a discussion of their Negro portraits would not add significantly to the understanding of Faulkner's methods of characterization. Some general comment though should be made about several of the characters in the novels that are not discussed. The Negro maid in *Pylon* is worthy of mention because she is one of Faulkner's faithful servants and is not without the tenderness and compassion that is characteristic of this group of Negro women. The Negro groomsman in *A Fable* possesses most of the Faulkner virtues. He is especially significant because it is through him that Faulkner makes clear the moral principles that underlie the central action of the story. He has learned "to believe and to hope", and he is able to communicate this idealism to others. He displays it first in his devotion to a maimed horse who wins races with only three legs and again in his concern to stop young men from dying in war. Perhaps one of the most delightfully humorous scenes in Faulkner's recent novels is the portrait of Aunt Het who defies the Snopes mule in *The Town.* In the group of novels that tell the Snopes's story the most significant statement about Negroes is contained in *The Mansion.* This comment explains the reaction of the Negro community to Linda Snopes's efforts to improve the quality of Negro schools and to exact some measure of social justice for the Negroes of Jefferson from the town officials. In this novel Faulkner explains that the Negro is aware of what he may expect from the white man and that he is aware of what he can contribute to white men. Generally Faulkner does not show great tolerance for the educated Negro, particularly for the Negro who is educated outside of the South. Although there is evidence that this is his attitude, the discussion in *The Mansion* shows respect for the educated Negro and briefly introduces for the first time, possibly, in Faulkner's fiction an educated Negro man. There are also in this novel two other Negro characters who should be mentioned. The Negro maid from Miss Reba's whore house is met again here. Her character is not different from what it was in *Sanctuary* but its quality is more carefully defined. She is one of Faulkner's "poor sons of bitches", a phrase which Faulkner uses in *The Mansion* to show his sympathy for the dilemma of all mankind; the term is equally applicable to all of the characters in the novel — to Mink Snopes, Linda Snopes, and Gavin Stevens. The second Negro character, the woman who comforts the whore during the church service, is important because she contributes to our understanding of Faulkner's attitude toward the church, perhaps to a definition of the church's proper place in society. Mink Snopes questions her presence at the worship service and is told that she belongs in the same sense that the others who are there belong. The glimpse given of her is brief but definitive. She is useful and kind. Most portraits of Negro characters in all of Faulkner's novels treat some aspect of the problem that he is concerned with in the portrait of Lucas.

Negro characters fulfill four functions in *Soldiers' Pay*, *Sartoris*, and *Sanctuary*. They give verisimilitude to the scenes, illustrate the social thesis, establish tone, atmosphere, and pace; and provide choric comment on the behavior of the white characters. The Negroes in these novels are minor characters who are frequently not essential to the plot. Often they are nameless and appear only once or twice. This is especially true of those in *Soldiers' Pay*.

In *Soldiers' Pay*, Faulkner gives us the names of two Negroes, Callie and her grandson Loosh, a veteran of the First World War. Callie was Donald Mahon's childhood nurse; and when he is brought home to die, she goes to visit him and takes Loosh with her. Very little is seen of Callie, but enough to show that she, like Elnora and Louvinia, is one of Faulkner's faithful servants. He handles her devotion to Donald respectfully and tenderly. One of the white characters says in praise of her: "Aunt Callie has raised more children than I can count. If she says he's sick, he is sick".[200] Loosh is close to a caricature. He wears a private's uniform, but he calls himself a corporal when he salutes Donald, who is blind. His grandmother refuses to allow him to practice duplicity with Donald. Loosh is stupid and comic. Three other Negroes are identified in the novel, a porter, a chauffeur, and a cornetist who leads the band at the country club dance. The solicitous care that the unnamed porter gives to Donald while he is in the train is carefully recorded. Faulkner says he was efficient and skillful.

The pace of the novel, at times, is set by the Negro characters. The

200 William Faulkner, *Soldiers' Pay* (New York, 1926), p. 262.

cornetist and his "sweating crew" established and controlled the movement of the dancers at the country club while they were on the dance floor and while the musicians rested. The story takes place in the summer. Faulkner attempts to show the effects of the weather and the tension of personal problems as they combine to create the novel's sensuous overripe atmosphere. He uses his Negro characters to help in doing this.

Gilligan, for example, has been studying Mrs. Powers's superiority and is acutely conscious of wanting her. Earlier, when he was about to overtake her in the street, "a Negro driving a wagon passed between them, interminable as Time":[201] Gilligan thought the wagon would never pass, so he darted around it in order to overtake the woman. When he does come up to her in the street, he feels that he and she are "lapped, surrounded, submerged by the frank odour of unwashed Negroes".[202] Gilligan is not at ease. When a Negro calls him, he swears and snaps at him. " 'Letter for you' replied the Negro equably, shaming him with better breeding".[203] When Mrs. Powers has left him, he is aware of the Negroes in the streets and of what Faulkner calls "the stolid coagulation of Negroes". In the street he sees Negroes driving mules. Beginning at this point of his awareness of the outside world and of his sense of frustration, Faulkner allows him to think: "Niggers and mules. Afternoon lay in a coma in the street like a woman recently loved. Quiet and warm: nothing now that the lover has gone away. Leaves were like a green liquid arrested in mid-flow, flattened and spread; leaves were as though cut with scissors from green paper and pasted flat on the afternoon: someone dreamed them and forgot his dream. Niggers and mules".[204] This impressionistic passage is followed by one that begins realistically, but trails off into impressionism:

Monotonous wagons drawn by long-eared beasts crawled past. [Notice how this sentence seems to establish the rhythm of the day.] Negroes humped with sleep, portentous upon each wagon and in the wagon bed itself sat other Negroes upon chairs: a pagan catafalque under the afternoon. Rigid as though carved in Egypt ten-thousand years ago. Slow dust rising veiled passing like time; the necks of mules limber as rubber hose swayed their heads from side to side, looking behind them always. But the mules were asleep also. "Ketch me sleep, he kill me. But I got mule blood in me: When he sleep, I sleep. When he wake, I wake".[205]

The two passages are used by Faulkner to describe the quality and passing of time. Gilligan's boredom, unrest, frustration are made real because of

[201] *Ibid.*, p. 141.
[202] *Ibid.*
[203] *Ibid.*, p. 143.
[204] *Ibid.*, p. 148.
[205] *Ibid.*

their existence in time. Their quality is made clear through the imagery of the passage. In the imagery Negroes and mules are used as symbols of survival and continuity. The statement that the mule driver makes does not mean that Negroes are less human. It is the kind of boasting that a folk hero does. This section of the novel ends, "The afternoon dreamed on toward sunset. Niggers and Mules. . . . At last Gilligan broke the silence".[206] In another passage, a continually moving line of Negroes carries "boards up a cleated incline like a chicken run into a freight car" and fling them to the floor. Their movement also establishes a pattern, "the slow reverberations of the cast boards smote at measured intervals".[207]

Most of the unidentified Negroes who are mentioned in the novel are observed while they move, usually up and down streets. Faulkner describes their movement before he makes other comments about them. This is a description of Negro school children:

Along the street passed slowly the hourly quota of Negro children who, seeming to have no arbitrary hours, seemingly free of all compulsions of time or higher learning, went to and from school at any hour possible . . . carrying lunch pails of ex-molasses and lard tins. Some of them also carried books. The lunch was usually eaten on the way to school, which was conducted by a foolish Negro in a lawn tie and an Alpaca coat.[208]

In addition to its contribution to pace and movement, this particular passage reflects what seems to be a less than sympathetic attitude toward formal education for Negroes. The realism is close to satire. The man who "conducted" the school may remind the reader of Fonsiba's husband, in "The Bear", whose formal education did not aid him in practical living.

The unhurried pace of Negro life becomes a kind of counterpoint to the murky intensity of some of the white lives. The Negro chauffeur wakes up briefly to make an accurate comment on the dress of women and falls asleep again.[209] There is the Negro boy who falls asleep "immediately like a horse" while he watches Gilligan's bags.[210] In another place a Negro "informal in his undershirt restrained his lawn mower" and stood in the shade of a tree and talked across the fence to a woman.[211] The Negros are unhurried, but, like the cornetist's musicians, they are an "indefatigable pack".

It should be remembered that Gilligan, who observes most often and comments on the behavior of Negroes in this novel, is a Northerner and that his awareness and contact with Negroes is fresh. "The hand of little employment

[206] *Ibid.*, p. 150.
[207] *Ibid.*, p. 155.
[208] *Ibid.*, p. 111.
[209] *Ibid.*, p. 209.
[210] *Ibid.*, p. 308.
[211] *Ibid.*, p. 180.

has the daintier sense!" Through him the reader is made aware of the paradox of the Negro's existence in the South. His first knowledge of Negro life in the South comes in the novel when a man says to the sheriff, "Well, I hear you killed a nigger yesterday". And he said, "Yes, weighed two hundred pounds. Like a bear".[212] Throughout the novel there is a contrast of what Gilligan hears about Negroes and what he sees of them. Before he leaves the town to return to the North, he attempts to summarize his knowledge of them. He says Negroes do what white people tell them, but that at the same time they make them feel immature, "Like you was a kid or something and that they'd look after you even if you don't know exactly what you want".[213] It is the Negroes who sing in their rude church and who provide for Gilligan, through the emotional quality of their singing, a spiritual contrast to the hardship of their daily lives, an understanding of the experiences that he has had in the town.[214] It is also with a description of the varied quality of their singing and a discussion of the paradoxes that form their lives that Faulkner ends the novel.

In *Sartoris*, Negroes are more precisely individualized characters than they are in *Soldiers' Pay*. The Sartoris family servants, Simon, Elnora, Caspey, and Isom (a family unit themselves) are carefully portrayed. In addition to these there are Houston, Rachel, Richard, the MacCullum Negroes, the blacksmith, John Henry and his family, the women in Mrs. Benbow's kitchen, and the musicians. There are several carefully planned "Negro" episodes, each extending over several pages: Simon goes to bring Miss Jenny, a Sartoris woman, home from a card party; and while he waits for her, he flirts with the mulatto maid who is serving and who is later to be the cause of his death. Caspey returns from the Army, tells his family about his experiences, describes his new-found lack of respect for white authority, and finally is knocked down (put in his place) by Colonel Sartoris. The behavior of the Negro musicians who provide the music for Bayard's drunken round of serenading forms one of these episodes. In another, Simon, who is the treasurer of the Negro church, gives the money entrusted to his care by the church to the young mulatto woman, and persuades Colonel Sartoris to protect the family honor by paying back the money he has stolen. One of the most satisfactory episodes is that in which John Henry persuades his family, his two brothers and his father, to rescue Bayard from the car that he has wrecked in a creek. The reactions of the Negro family with whom Bayard almost forcibly spends Christmas eve and Christmas form another episode.

[212] *Ibid.*, p. 2.
[213] *Ibid.*, p. 309.
[214] *Ibid.*, pp. 325–326.

The Sartoris family servants are portrayed through the way they do their household tasks. Elnora is competent. She works in the kitchen, often without her shoes, and she sings while she works. She is not developed in detail, nor is she made a comic character as her father, brother, and son are. Simon, Elnora's father, drives the Sartoris carriage and is the butler. His understanding of the Sartoris family is complete and penetrating, but his personal behavior is comic and often stupid. Simon is aware of manners and ceremony, but these no longer have a place in his world. When he uses them, they are an empty flourish, crude and ludicrous. He is a caricature of his former useful self. In this respect Simon may be compared with Rachel, Belle's cook. Rachel is saved from Simon's fate because of her usefulness. She is the best cook in town.[215] It is difficult not to call Simon a stereotype, and this can be avoided only if it is understood that the decay of the Sartoris family parallels Simon's behavior. Simon's status is dependent upon the status of the Sartoris family. The decline of the family and the shift to a machine civilization has made Simon's function as carriage driver almost useless. Simon is forced to pretend, to clown, in order to give meaning and dignity to the things he must do. It is no longer possible for him to dignify his job. Most of the time, his top hat and his duster, the symbols of his former usefulness, hang in the carriage house and gather dust, while his prized carriage horses wander about the pasture, eating and getting fat.

Isom, Elnora's son, who works the flowers in Miss Jenny's garden, is a child. He is alert and curious when there is an opportunity to ride in Bayard's car, but his greatest skill is displayed in avoiding the work Miss Jenny tells him to do. Miss Jenny says he made his living by being born black.

Caspey works on the farm. He returned from the first World War with a number of "uppity" ideas about Negro rights. Miss Jenny says that she agrees with Mr. Vardaman that it was a mistake to send Negroes to war.[216] Caspey lies about his experiences in the Army and tries to impress his family that he was a hero. His attitude is corrected by Colonel Sartoris, who knocks him down when he hesitates to obey an order to saddle his horse. Caspey's treatment indicates Faulkner's attitude toward social justice for Negroes as they attempt to seek it for themselves. Perhaps this attitude is responsible for the characterization of Loosh, the Negro soldier in *Soldiers' Pay*.

The life of the Negro in the town parallels the life of the white man. Simon's class is disappearing because the class to which the Sartorises belong is disappearing. The commercial class, represented in its most sinister manifestation by the Snopeses, is thriving. What Simon derisively calls "town niggers"

[215] *Sartoris*, p. 191.
[216] *Ibid.*, p. 167.

as a class are thriving. There are Negro stores. Melony, the girl who attracts Simon and leads to his ruin, opens a beauty parlor, perhaps with the money that Simon steals from the church.

In this novel, Faulkner gives careful attention to the details that reveal the manners and customs of a particular region. He notices the way the Negro characters walk, the kinds of clothes they wear, the effects of perspiration upon these clothes, their behavior in the presence of white people; he records details of this kind with a convincing accuracy. Frequently the details of social behavior, through the pattern that is observable in them, reveal the superficial nature of many of the regional conventions.

Negroes and whites, for example, do not usually eat and drink together. However, Bayard and the MacCullum boy drink with Houston, the Negro waiter, who served them in the back room of the restaurant.[217] When Bayard goes serenading, he takes a cup along for the Negro musicians to drink from; but when he becomes drunk, they drink from the jug with him.[218] The Negro family that is Bayard's unwilling host on Christmas day drank with him. "The Negroes drank with him, amicably, a little diffidently — two opposed concepts antipathetic by race, blood, nature and environment, touching for a moment and fused within an illusion — human kind forgetting its lust and cowardice and guilt for a day. "Chris'mus" the woman murmured shyly. 'Thanky, suh' ".[219]

Most of the Negro characters clearly make an effort to stay out of "white folks affairs". The couple into whose home Bayard forced himself on Christmas illustrate this through their reluctance to have him as a guest. Elnora hesitates to tell Colonel Sartoris and Miss Jenny things that she knows are of importance to them and to the well-being of the family. This fear of interference is well illustrated when John Henry's family rescues Bayard from the wreckage of his car and saves him from drowning in the creek. Bayard failed in one of his daredevil stunts and crashed his car nose-down in a creek. John Henry, a Negro youth, was driving with his brothers and their father in their wagon along the same road. They argue among themselves for some time before they decide to leave the wagon and have a look at the accident. They hesitated not because of a lack of humanity, but because they feared they might be accused of having had some part in the accident. From the position of Bayard's body they judged that he was dead. If he was not dead, he might die while they were trying to take him where he could be helped; and they might be accused of contributing to the cause of his death. For this reason the father felt that they should not move the body. The pace of

[217] *Ibid.*, pp. 122, 126.
[218] *Ibid.*, p. 157.
[219] *Ibid.*, pp. 341–350.

the episode is slow and halting. Reluctance characterizes the action. In the end, John Henry's humanity is stronger than his fear, and he persuades his family to rescue Bayard; but the process is not an easy one.[220]

Faulkner's treatment of miscegenation is remarkably different from that of many authors who write on this subject. He does not make his mulattoes tragic because of their white blood, or pathetic because of their black blood, nor does he find that mixed blood makes them superior. His treatment of race, if his work is considered as a whole, is social; and his conclusions are based on pragmatic findings. Most of his studies of miscegenation are examinations of the connotative meanings of the word Negro and illustrations of the compulsive force of those meanings in the determination of social attitudes. He describes the particular unions that produced mulattoes, and he lists the particular sets of social factors that led to these unions and that conditioned the development of the offspring. Given the social situation of the South, Faulkner feels that miscegenation was inevitable. As a whole, the treatment that he has given the problem is ethical and derives its central values from Faulkner's attitude toward the presence of the two evils in the South. It is suggested in the introductory section of this essay that Lucas Beauchamp is Faulkner's definitive and inclusive portrait of the Negro. And as Lucas illustrates Faulkner's attitude toward other Negro problems, from the point of view of the individual adjusting within the society, he also illustrates that attitude toward miscegenation. Lucas is a person who experiences no social or psychological conflict because of his mixed blood. Ideally all mulattoes should achieve Lucas's adaptation within the society. Their failure to do this is a means that Faulkner uses to show the compulsive force of the connotative meanings of the word Negro and his means of commenting on the social and ethical implications of race.

Through Joe Christmas, Faulkner investigates the social responses of an individual and the people around him to the connotative meanings of "Negro".

The thirty-three years of Joe's life are divided into four unequal time periods: five years in the orphanage, thirteen years with the McEacherns, twelve years in "the street", and three years with Miss Burden. The first eighteen years of his life are a formative period whose pattern is determined, Richard Chase believes, in the orphanage, "When the dietitian finds that he has been hiding in her closet eating tooth paste while she was entertaining an interne on her bed".[221]

Joe's character may be said to develop until he leaves the McEacherns

[220] *Ibid.*, pp. 305–315.
[221] Richard Chase, "The Stone and The Crucifixion; Faulkner's *Light in August*", *The Kenyon Review*, X (Autumn 1948), 544.

to enter "the street" and by choice accepts the compulsive pattern of flight and pursuit. The entry into "the street", Joe's refusal to accept the burden of his humanity — his search for and flight from selfhood — ends the development of his character. After this point in the novel his character is revealed rather than developed. The four periods as they are portrayed through the plot and structure of the novel reveal the struggle for dominance of two concepts existing side by side in Joe's mind.

Richard Chase says: "In *Light in August*, Faulkner seems to be concerned with showing that the codes modern man *does* set up do *not* allow him to define himself as human — that codes have become compulsive patterns which man clings to in fear and trembling while the pattern emasculates him".[222] The connotations of "Negro" are the basis of a myth-like body of attitudes that form the racial codes in Southern (and to some extent in American) society and that compulsively determine social behavior between the races. The inter-personal behavior between individuals and between groups of individuals is in one sense, therefore, a separation of man by language. "There is never any real proof that Joe is part Negro, but Joe's gratuitous assumption is at the root of all his actions".[223] He is called a nigger when he is a child, and he learns the connotations of the word. From those connotations the compulsive pattern of his life is formed. The individual who is Joe Christmas is submerged beneath the social being that a word connotes. The social significance of this fact is that an individual (and Faulkner seems to think that Joe's case is typical in this respect) is shadowed by evils inherited from a pre-Civil War ideology. So it is that when Faulkner develops the character of Joe Christmas, translates the problem of race into flesh and blood, he handles at the same time the problem of evil. He, in fact, calls Joe's story "the mechanics, the theatring of evil".[224]

The theatrics of evil is worked out through Joe in a conflict, as Chase suggests, between modernism and holistic consciousness. Joe refuses to consider marrying Miss Burden, accepting a holistic pattern of living comparable to that elected by Byron Bunch, because such a marriage will destroy the thing that he has deliberately made himself. Joe has consciously rejected the burden of his humanity, has consciously made himself into a version of the city man, symbolized in his choice of clothes, and has deliberately chosen not to be an individual. Faulkner finds man's efforts not to bear the burden of his humanity evil, and so the theatrics of evil can be seen in Joe's pathological struggles with himself.

The connotations of Negro that are dramatically portrayed in the personal

[222] *Ibid.*, p. 543.
[223] *Ibid.*, p. 546.
[224] William Faulkner, *Light in August* (New York, 1932), p. 244.

and inter-personal aspects of Joe's life may perhaps be made clearer in their mode of operation through the story "Elly".[225] Elly's instincts drive her to seek sexual satisfaction with a young man of her acquaintance. To satisfy this desire and to accept the consequences of her action would be bearing the burden of her humanity. Lena Burch, who represents Faulkner's concept of holistic consciousness, does this. Elly shares the knowledge of her desire with a friend who challenges her: "You didn't notice his hair then. Like a knitted cap. And his lips. Blubber almost".[226] The connotations of Negro are implied in the description. The social code that Elly accepts is brought into conflict with her natural desires. The man who stimulated those desires is not changed, but the connotations of the word Negro embodied in the code are compulsive. Elly's instincts triumph first, but not for long. The code drives her to arrange the death of herself and her lover. In a similar manner the connotative value of the label Negro determines the actions, not only of Joe, but of the people around him.

The people of Jefferson, for example, believed that Miss Burden's murder was "committed not by a negro but by Negro".[227] When speaking to Joe of her attitude toward race, Miss Burden contributes to the connotative meaning of Negro: "I seemed to see them [Negroes] for the first time not as people, but as a thing, a shadow in which I lived, we lived, all white people all other people lived. I thought of all the children coming forever and forever into the world, white, with the black cross falling upon them before they drew breath. And I seemed to see the black shadow in the shape of a cross".[228] In this novel the white characters regard Negroes as different from other people perhaps as a kind of burden that they must bear. Miss Burden's name is significant in this respect. Each race fears the other, and the fear and the tensions produced by it give connotations to the word Negro. The particular connotation of Negro to Miss Burden, in fact, is responsible for her failure as a person. Hines developed a phobia-like attitude toward Negroes that progressed to insanity. His phobia is determined by the connotation rather than by the denotation of the word. The chauvinism that colors Percy Grimm's actions is also influenced by the connotations of the word. The special meaning of the word materializes in the dietitian's mind when she becomes aware than an adequate and suitable punishment for Joe and revenge for herself is to send him to the nigger orphanage. "He will look just like a pea in a pan full of coffee beans", she thinks.[229] The dietitian does not believe that Joe is a Negro. He is a child whom she fears as if he were an adult.

[225] "Elly", *Doctor Martino*, pp. 242–262.
[226] *Ibid.*, p. 245.
[227] *Light in August*, p. 271.
[228] *Ibid.*, p. 239.
[229] *Ibid.*, p. 122.

Her actions toward him are produced by her fear and her effort to protect herself. This same connotative meaning of the word Negro causes the matron of the orphanage to decide that they must find people to adopt Joe immediately. Max makes use of these meanings when he calls Joe the play-boy of Beale Street. It is these connotative meanings that enable the man who observes Joe when he is captured in Mottstown to say that he didn't act like a nigger and he didn't act like a white person.[230]

At the planing mill, the men who have been baffled and offended by Joe's aloofness, by his name, and foreign appearance find these things satisfactorily explained when they are told that he is a Negro. Joe uses the word as a weapon to hurt the white women with whom he has been intimate. He is so certain of its effectiveness as a weapon that when it fails him, when he discovers that there are white women who do have relations with Negro men without re-pugnance, he is "sick" for two years.[231]

The employment of the connotative rather than the denotative meaning of the word produces the tragedy in the novel. The characters have divorced ideas from fact. This separation results in human wrongs and in the failure of human beings to accept human responsibilities. Joe's problem is purely a mental one. By choice he can be white or black (or neither). When he is captured in Mottstown, he is a man, not a Negro or white man.[232] Lucas Beauchamp avoids Joe's problem by consciously being neither white nor black, but an individual. But Joe is never able to make a choice. The social meanings of the two terms that designate race set up emotional responses in him that prevent his making a choice. Joe is not unaware of his problem. Ap-parently it has clear definition in his mind. As he defines it, he is searching for peace. Like Conrad's Lord Jim, Joe is an isolated individual; but unlike him, he is never able to accept his humanity, to immerse himself in the destructive element. To the extent that the search for self-hood and the awareness of isolation are a part of each human existence, Joe is Everyman.[233]

The conflict within Joe Christmas is like the conflict between white and Negro people in the South, embodying within a single individual the problem of a region. Joe is a metaphorical expression of the South's dilemma. Thus, he is neither black nor white, but two opposing concepts, each seeking exist-ence, if not dominance, in the same area. Joe can also logically be interpreted as an allegorical figure who symbolizes man's refusal to bear the burden of his humanity and the destruction or evil that results from such refusal. Joe's attitude toward himself and the attitude of white and Negro people toward

---

[230] *Ibid.*, p. 331.
[231] *Ibid.*, p. 212.
[232] *Ibid.*, p. 331.
[233] Phyllis Hirshleifer, "As Whirlwinds in the South: An Analysis of *Light in August*", *Perspective*, II (Summer 1949), 225–238.

him represent a particular psychology, a psychology growing out of the South's twin evils.

Joe Christmas thinks that he is a mulatto, but his thinking lacks the support of evidence. Joe believes he is part Negro, because he remembers being called a Negro and being treated in a special way while he was in the orphanage. After the orphanage period, the first five years of his life, twelve years pass before he is called a Negro again. From the time that he is eighteen until the day of his capture for the murder of Miss Burden in Mottstown, he is never called a Negro except by people whom he has told that he has mixed blood. There is no proof in the novel that Joe is part Negro. His maternal grandfather, Hines, has only the word of the circus manager (who employed Joe's father) and his own demented intuition, as proof that Joe's father was part Negro and not Mexican. It is a fact that Joe is darker than some of the children in the orphanage, that many of the people who see him describe him as "foreign looking". Other white people, however, say of him that "He looks as white as I do".

Joe believes that he is part Negro. "If I'm not, damned if I haven't wasted a lot of time", he tells Miss Burden.[234] This is the idea that Faulkner develops in the chapters dealing with Joe's childhood and maturity. "Memory believes before knowing remembers".[235] This fact is basic to an understanding of Joe's behavior. Joe's attitude toward his race is a survival of his experiences in the orphanage. The children and the dietitian called him a nigger. Hines watched him when he was on the playground; and although he said only a few words to him, Joe remembered their impression: " 'Why dont you play with them other children like you used to do?' And he [Joe] didn't say nothing and old Doc Hines said, 'Do you think you are a nigger?' and he didn't say nothing and old Doc Hines said, 'Do you think you are a nigger because God has marked your face?' And he said 'Is God a nigger too?' "[236] Because he was left alone and called a nigger by the other children, Joe became curious about the Negro yardman and watched and questioned him: " 'How come you are a nigger?' and the nigger said, 'Who told you I am a nigger, you little white trash bastard?' and he said 'I aint a nigger', and the nigger says, 'You are worse than that. You dont know what you are. And more than that you wont never know. You'll live and you'll die and you wont never know' ".[237] The lack of knowledge that the Negro mentions is the core of the problem that Joe faces throughout his life. As a child he must believe that the other children and the adults have some reason for calling him a "nigger" and behaving as they do

---

[234] *Light in August*, p. 241.
[235] *Ibid.*, p. 11.
[236] *Ibid.*, p. 362.
[237] *Ibid.*, p. 363.

toward him. His memories of childhood are his only proof that he is a Negro. When he is older, he believes even though he has no proof.

The twelve years that Joe spent as the adopted son of the McEacherns formed and crystalized his character. While he was with them, the five years of orphanage experience were not "sloughed off". They became, as a matter of fact, his guide for understanding and interpreting experience. Although he had no external contacts that caused him to wonder if he was part Negro, he continued to think that he was. During these years he tested in his mind the possibility of using his claim to Negro blood as a means of hurting others. At least once he thought of hurting McEachern in this way. In the same way he clung to his name in spite of McEachern's exclamation, "Christmas". "A heathenish name. Sacrilege. I will change that".[238] Actually McEachern changed very few, if any, of Joe's characteristics. Fatalism may be regarded as an aspect of McEachern's Presbyterianism, but Joe's fatalism had become a part of his acceptance of life before he left the orphanage. He admired McEachern's Presbyterian inflexibility, because in contrast to the dietitian's behavior, it was always predictable and unwavering. Correspondingly, he rejected the kindness and starved affection of Mrs. McEachern because she was unpredictable. The instinct that causes Joe to withdraw from the group at the orphanage develops and asserts itself in his desire for social approval which leads to conflicts with McEachern, to an adolescent curiosity about women, and to the relation with Bobbie. This desire for social approval is evidence of pride and vanity, and it marks Joe as a social being rather than as an individual. Joe searches for individuality, but his desire for social approval makes difficult and frustrates this search.

Joe's loss of innocence through the love affair with Bobbie and the shattering of the illusion upon which the love affair was built are perhaps the most significant events in his life with the McEacherns. Joe falls in love with Bobbie, although his experiences with women, the dietitian, Mrs. McEachern, and the Negro with whom he tried unsuccessfully to lose his virtue, have been unpleasant. Joe's love for Bobbie is based upon illusion and ignorance. He is aware of his ignorance and ashamed of it, but he expects to learn. Ignorance is also the source of his illusion about the true nature of the woman he loves. A person of more experience would have known from a first meeting what Bobbie was and what she had been. When Joe does learn these things, his lack of experience and his physical passion prevent him from realizing their significance. His lack of experience is coupled with his desire for social approval, and Bobbie, through the aid of Max and Mame, opens up a new world of experiences and attitudes for him. He is a clod hopper. They are city people. When they talked, "It was as if they talked at and because of him, in a language which he did not understand".[239] Max and Mame are examples of Modernism, and they influence Joe to accept their way of life and to reject the holistic consciousness that might have developed him into an individual.

Bobbie is sick at their first meeting, and Joe learns with a disgust that lessens into tolerance that the rumor of woman's periodic sickness that he has partially verified by killing and examining a female sheep is true. He discovers later that he is not the only man who visits Bobbie in her room. Again disgust is followed by acceptance and not only acceptance, but by an effort to make himself into the kind of man that the men who visit Bobbie are. He is aware that his love is degrading, for he calls his visits to Bobbie sin and thinks of the rope that he uses to leave the McEachern window as an implement of sin.[240] His moral degeneration, or social adaptation, for one accomplishes the other, is rapid. In two weeks, once he is admitted to the society of the men who visit Max's home, he learns to smoke and drink. He wears his hat, smokes his cigarette, and talks as the other men do. During this period, before the men whose approval he desires, he calls Bobbie his whore. Consciously, he was transforming himself into a variety of the city man that he was to be for the rest of his life.

The knowledge that Bobbie is a prostitute does not change Joe's feelings for her. His behavior toward her reflects his understanding of the decorum of the group whose approval he desires, but his feelings remain as they were at the beginning of the relation. His plan to marry her is evidently not a sudden thought, inspired on the night of the dance when he struck and killed McEachern. If the plan for marriage had not been made earlier than this night, Joe would no doubt have understood the change in Bobbie's affection that was apparent after McEachern attacked them on the dance floor. She blames Joe for the things that McEachern called her. Already she has turned against Joe, but he does not realize this. Obviously, the illusion, the condition that made his love possible, was a deep one.

When Bobbie refuses to go away with him, his illusion is broken, and his innocence is destroyed. The loss of innocence, the sense of sin, provide a need to search for salvation. Essentially, this is what the period in "the street" may be called. The experiences that come to Joe on the night that Bobbie rejects his love and returns to Memphis, leaving him beaten and dazed on the floor of Max's abandoned house, set Joe upon the street. The experiences come to Joe at a time when he has consciously prepared himself to give up the

---

239 *Ibid.*, p. 190.
240 *Ibid.*, p. 179.

way of life that McEachern offered him and when he has consciously selected another. The experiences include the murder of the man who had reared him, and who according to his own bigoted sense of values had dealt predictably and justly, if not kindly, with him. He discovers that Bobbie does not love him. "Bastard! Son of a Bitch!" she says. "Getting me into a jam, that always treated you like you were a white man. A white man!"[241] Joe is not prepared for this: "He just stared at her, at the face which he had never seen before, saying quietly (whether aloud or not, he could not have said) in a slow amazement: *Why, I committed murder for her. I even stole for her* as if he had just heard of it, thought of it, been told that he had done it".[242] In addition to committing murder and stealing for Bobbie, Joe is beaten because of her and left bloody and senseless on the floor when Bobbie leaves the house with Max and Mame.

The racial aspect of Joe's problem is made clear through the women in his life. Joe tells Bobbie that he has Negro blood, not to hurt her, but because he loved her and wanted her to know everything about him. Her reaction to this information does not disturb him. During the period that he lives with the McEacherns, the only time that the reader discovers any attitude or feeling in Joe toward the possibility of his having Negro blood is in a moment of disgust with Mrs. McEachern when he thought to tell her, "I dare you to tell him what he has nursed. That he has nursed a nigger beneath his own roof, with his own food at his own table".[243] After Bobbie has deserted Joe, when he associates with white women, if he can pay them he does not tell them that he is part Negro. On such occasions, it may be assumed that the act and the payment are sufficient to satisfy Joe's egotism and to protect his status. On the other hand, when he cannot pay, he tells the women that he is part Negro. Inability to pay denies him social approval; but when the woman is told that he is part Negro, her embarrassment and sense of anger and shame because of her defilement are perhaps a compensation for Joe. The occasion when Joe does not pay illustrates the connotative value of the word Negro. There are times when "he was beaten unconscious by other patrons, to waken in the street or in jail".[244] During this same period, he tricked or teased white men into calling him a Negro in order to fight them, to beat them or to be beaten.[245]

By this time, at least, the problem of being white or black has certainly established itself. Joe's actions now begin to reflect the influence of the

[241] *Ibid.*, p. 204.
[242] *Ibid.*
[243] *Ibid.*, p. 157.
[244] *Ibid.*, p. 210.
[245] *Ibid.*, p. 211.

prevailing social attitudes toward race. Unlike the aspects of his character that are discernible during his first eighteen years, this one does not develop before the reader's eyes. Faulkner reveals it in a full intensity, as if it had always been a part of Joe's personality structure. The things that may have contributed to its nurture and growth are there also, so that, while a reader may have some curiosity about the progress of its development, he is not surprised to discover, or rather to be told, that it exists.

In his search for peace Joe moves from one woman to another, but his relations with them are seldom perfectly honest. He seems always "doomed" to conceal something from them. This concealment, no doubt, is an expression of his wish to be an individual, while the manner in which he conducts his relations with women may be thought of as designed to produce social approval. This is illustrated in his affair with Miss Burden. Joe's pride and vanity will not allow him to let Brown or any other man know what his relation with Miss Burden has become. He does not object to the perverseness of the relation, but to the public opinion of it. In the orphanage he conceals from the dietitian that he is eating her toothpaste. He steals money from Mrs. McEachern, and he rewards her proffered affections with subterfuge and rebuffs. He never tells Bobbie where the money came from that he gave her. He does not tell Miss Burden that he sells whiskey on her property.

As Joe moves from one place to another and from one woman to another, it seems that his failure to end his physical desires is a symbol of his failure to find peace or to find selfhood. The women in fact seem to "surround" him and to prevent him from achieving success in his search. He had hated Mrs. McEachern because of "that soft kindness which he believed himself doomed to be forever victim of and which he hated worse than he did the hard ruthless justice of men".[246] His attitude toward the women is paradoxical. He seeks them, but once he has established a relation with one, he wants to be free of her. Joe's problem is one that has to be resolved on the mental level, but he tries to externalize it through the conflict of sexual conquest. The kind of stories that he reads and the method that he follows in reading them offer some evidence of this. The covers of the magazines that he reads bear "pictures of young women in underclothes or men in the act of shooting one another with pistols".[247] It is his habit to read the magazines straight through and to destroy them when he is finished. After Bobbie and before Miss Burden this is what he does figuratively with women. He becomes afraid of Miss Burden when he cannot abandon her.

Joe finds women to be unpredictable, and it is this characteristic in them

[246] *Ibid.*, p. 158.
[247] *Ibid.*, p. 104.

that he resents most. Mrs. McEachern is unpredictable in contrast to her husband, whose actions are unvarying. When Joe is caught in the dietitian's closet, he expects to be spanked for stealing her toothpaste; and when the punishment he expects does not come, he is puzzled. Bobbie, like the dietitian and Mrs. McEachern, is also unpredictable. She turns against him after he has made sacrifices for her. The women between Bobbie and Miss Burden are also unpredictable; one so much so that when he tells her that he is part Negro, she is not affected. Joe is defenseless against this unpredictability. Miss Burden is perhaps the most unpredictable of the women who come into Joe's life. His association with her is divided into three phases, each of which is different and a surprise to Joe.

The period of association with Miss Burden is different from the period of the street. In a way it is comparable to the period with Bobbie. Bobbie opens up and makes acceptable to Joe new experiences of life. Miss Burden carries the experiences to their ugliest extremity and closes forever the escape that Bobbie had opened for Joe. But at the same time she is the means of Joe's discovery of himself. Miss Burden understands Joe's problem; and although she is unpredictable as the other women in his life are, she is different from them. Her own problem is somewhat like Joe's. She has come to think of the Negro as a burden that she must bear. Joe also bears this burden. She bears it willingly and manfully. At best Joe bears it unwillingly. The Negro makes Miss Burden a social outsider. Joe's attitude toward the possibility of having Negro blood makes him an outsider. Each of them has failed as a person: Miss Burden through an altruistic self-abnegation and devotion to abstract principle; Joe because of a refusal to recognize himself and to accept himself.

Joe's relationship with Miss Burden is divided into three phases: "During the first phase it had been as though he were outside a house where snow was on the ground, trying to get into the house; during the second phase he was at the bottom of a pit in the hot wild darkness; now [in the third phase] he was in the middle of a plain where there was no house, not even snow, not even wind".[248] Each of these phases brings Joe closer to himself, and in this respect Miss Burden is the instrument of Joe's self-discovery. At the end of the first phase Joe learns that Miss Burden's problem is similar to his own. He learns this through the story of her family's existence in the South against the background of the relationship that they have begun.

Joe could not understand Miss Burden when he met her. Several times he thought of leaving her and entering "the street" again. As a woman she was unusual, and his association with her did not give him the satisfaction

248 *Ibid.*, pp. 254–255.

of conquest that he had grown accustomed to finding. Usually he has determined the pattern of his relationships with women, but his relation with Miss Burden is guided by her. It is her habit to leave food for him in the kitchen. One evening when he enters the house, the food that is set out for him seems to offer an explanation of her behavior. *"Set out for the nigger. For the nigger"*, he thinks.[249] Then he destroys the food, breaking the individual dishes on the floor. It is after this period in their relationship, his failure more or less to conquer Miss Burden as a woman, that he gets a job at the planing mill. His job interrupts their relationship until she comes to the cabin in which he lives and tells him about her family. He thinks that she has come to surrender to him as a woman. Instead it is her purpose to explain why she is in the South.

At the end of the Civil War her grandfather had brought their family into the South with the intention of helping the newly-freed slaves gain what he felt was rightfully theirs. Colonel John Sartoris had murdered her grandfather and her brother when they attempted to help Negroes participate in the local government of the town of Jefferson. At the time the story begins Miss Burden is left alone, an outsider, hated by the white people of Jefferson, still trying to improve the Negro. Joe learns from her recital how a particular concept of the Negro and of justice for the Negro came to dominate her life and her family's life and kept her from leading the life that a woman should lead. Miss Burden's life is an illustration of the compulsive force of the connotations of the word Negro. Significantly Joe asks Miss Burden: "Just when do men that have different blood stop hating one another?"[250] He is talking about the North and South, but the question may be asked about Negroes and whites, and it may be asked in a particular way about Joe, who has both these hates confined in himself.

The second phase of the relation began after Miss Burden had given Joe the history of her family and explained to him the task that her father had assigned her. Her father had told her: "You must struggle, rise. But in order to rise, you must raise the shadow [the Negro] with you. But you can never lift it to your level. I see that now, which I did not see until I came down here. But escape it you cannot. The curse of the black race is God's curse. But the curse of the white race is the black man who will be forever God's chosen own because he once cursed Him".[251] The things that Miss Burden has learned through her own experience in the South, primarily that she was an outsider and that she was a woman who had failed to fulfill her natural

[249] *Ibid.*, p. 224.
[250] *Ibid.*, p. 236.
[251] *Ibid.*, p. 240.

function, enable her to see the error in her father's judgment. The attitude of the white Southerner toward the Negro was wrong, but her father's attitude was not right.

Like Joe, Miss Burden has lived in a kind of street, cut off from life as it is represented by normal, or usual, human contacts. The beginning of a sexual relationship with Joe proves to her how much she has been cut off from the world. This same relationship is the means of her learning that it is too late for her to do anything about her wasted life. In evaluating her life Joe observes "the abnegation in it: the imperious and fierce urgency that concealed an actual despair at frustrate and irrevocable years, which she appeared to attempt to compensate for each night on earth by damning herself forever to the hell of her forefathers, by living not alone in sin but in filth".[252] During this phase she passed through every "avatar" of the woman in love. All of her life she had been obsessed with an erroneously conceived missionary zeal. During this phase her obsession seems to turn upon her and to cause her to concentrate all of her interests upon Joe in a kind of maniacal intensity. In her frenzy and desperation it seems that Joe has become not only her way of expressing herself as a woman, but also her last opportunity to follow her father's command to raise the Negro.

Joe becomes afraid and thinks of leaving. He notices that there are two creatures struggling in Miss Burden's body, as there are two concepts struggling in his mind: "Now it would be the still, cold, contained figure of the first phase who, even though lost and damned, remained somehow impervious and impregnable; then it would be the other ... who in furious denial of that impregnability strove to drown in the black abyss of its own creating that physical purity which had been preserved too long now even to be lost".[253] By studying Miss Burden and trying, although often failing, to understand her, Joe gets a clearer insight into his own problems.

Miss Burden talks to Joe about having a baby. For her this would be a means of carrying out the task assigned to her and a means of making up for the sin that she has committed with Joe. Joe misunderstands her talk about having a baby and thinks that it is a trap to persuade him to marry her. He thinks of the security and ease that marriage to her would mean, but he decides that he does not want these. "If I give in now, I will deny all the thirty years that I lived to make me what I chose to be".[254] This is the only time that Joe says that he is what he is by choice. The assertion is consistent with Faulkner's conception of free will. It also suggests an attitude

[252] *Ibid.*, p. 244.
[253] *Ibid.*, p. 246.
[254] *Ibid.*, pp. 250–251.

toward the evil that manifests itself in Joe. This evil is escapable, although Joe fails to escape it.

When Miss Burden is deluded into believing that she is going to have a baby, she tells Joe. As he has done before in similar cases, he plans to leave her; but he does not. This marks the beginning of the third period. It is during this period that Miss Burden tells Joe that he is wasting his life and proposes that he take part in the work that she is doing for Negroes. She plans for him to go to school. His response is "To school. . . . A nigger school. Me? Tell niggers that I am a nigger too?"[255] All of his life Joe has struggled against making a choice. Miss Burden's suggestion that he do so strikes at the center of his problem and hurts him. His retaliation is cruel: he calls her an old woman and tells her that she is not pregnant. During this moment each is revealed to the other for what he really is. Miss Burden strikes Joe a blow on the face that he returns. After the exchange of blows, Miss Burden evaluates their past and future lives by saying: "Maybe it would be better if we both were dead".[256] This is a prophetic statement, for they both will be dead in a few days.

Convinced that their relation is sinful, Miss Burden urges Joe to kneel and pray with her. He refuses to kneel, but he remains to listen to her pray. Her prayer is a confession of sin. Since a child did not result from her union with Joe, Miss Burden felt that that union represented waste, a misdirection of energy, a selfish expression of egotism, and was therefore sinful. The union itself had not been sinful, but its purpose and outcome had. She talked to God as if he were another man in a room with two men.[257] She was certain that her life was wasted, and she felt that she should be dead. On the night that Joe murders her, she tells him to kneel with her and says that it is not she who asks it. This implies the existence of some universal force that somehow judges the actions of man and charges man to pay a penalty when he is sinful. When Joe refuses to kneel with her, she draws a pistol; and if the bullet in its chamber had exploded, she would have killed him.

It is in this way that the third phase moves toward Joe's death and Miss Burden contributes to Joe's self-knowledge by showing him that he cannot go back to "the street". She convinces him that he has wasted his life, but he refuses to try to remedy this waste. She finally convinces him that death, since he does not have sufficient courage to live, is the only solution to his problem.

Joe's experiences with Negroes are usually abortive attempts to identify

[255] *Ibid.*, pp. 261-262.
[256] *Ibid.*, p. 263.
[257] *Ibid.*, p. 265.

himself with them. They reflect the compulsive force of the connotations of Negro. These experiences begin when as a child in the orphanage he becomes curious about the name he has been called. He follows a Negro workman about the grounds, observing and questioning him, attempting to identify himself with him, but the workman repulses his curiosity. The next encounter with a Negro comes when Joe is fourteen and seeking sexual initiation. Faulkner does not comment on the racial aspects of this encounter in a general way; but when Joe looked at the Negro girl that his friends and he had procured, it seemed to him that he was looking down into a dark abyss. This is much the same feeling that he has when he wears the Negro shoes just before his capture, or that he felt when he went into Freedman Town or desecrated the Negro church. The girl frightens Joe, and he does not attempt to identify himself with her.

When Joe associates with Negro women while he is in "the street", Faulkner says that he is sick. By *sick* Faulkner refers (it seems) to a mental condition rather than a physical one. Perhaps this period marks Joe's beginning awareness of the nature of the conflict in himself. This period lasts for two years. The sickness that affects Joe is the revulsion that the Southern white man may feel when he knows that his women have broken the racial sex taboo. His disgust as a white person is so great, that he seemingly decides that he will not be white. His effort to be a Negro during this period is concentrated and desperate. He apparently believes all of the things about Negroes that other white people believe about them. He believes these things about himself. This is what causes him to have so much difficulty in trying to be a Negro. There is in Joe the love of the self that is common to all men. The antagonism that is expressed against white people is probably expressed because he feels that they have made him what he is. To say the least, they make him conscious of being essentially different from themselves. His attacks upon white people are either conscious or unconscious defenses of his possible Negro blood. During this period he attempts to see white people as a Negro would see them. Inevitably, of course, he must hurt himself.

During this black period of his life in "the street," he lived:

As man and wife with a woman who resembled an ebony carving. At night he would lie in bed beside her, sleepless, beginning to breathe deep and hard. He would do it deliberately, feeling, even watching, his white chest arch deeper and deeper within his ribcage, trying to breathe into himself the dark odor, the dark and inscrutable thinking and being of Negroes, with each suspiration trying to expel from himself the white blood and the white thinking and being, and all the while his nostril at the odor which he was trying to make his own would whiten and tauten, his whole being writhe and strain with physical outrage and spiritual denial.[258]

During this period he fought Negroes who called him white or referred in any way to his whiteness.

The next significant encounters with Negroes came just before Joe has murdered Miss Burden. Miss Burden suggested that he become a Negro in fact, that he formally attach himself to the race. He refuses her suggestion with force and indignation, but the force of the refusal does not show that it is made with ease. After he leaves Miss Burden, seemingly under compulsion, he walks through Freedman Town. This is an indication that it was not easy for him to refuse Miss Burden's plan and that he knows in what way his life has been a failure. The walk through Freedman Town is intentional; perhaps it is an effort to see for the last time if he can endure being a Negro. Physically, Freedman Town is different from the other sections of the city. Once Joe is in the area he feels that Negro voices and smells enclose him. Without any contact with people, he becomes frightened:

As from the bottom of a thick black pit he saw himself inclosed by cabin shapes, vague kerosene lit, so that the street lamps themselves seemed to be further spaced, as if the black life, black breathing had compounded the substance of breath, so that not only voices but moving bodies and light itself must become fluid and accrete slowly from particle to particle, of and with the now ponderable night inseparable and one.[259]

Not only does Joe feel enclosed by the place but "On all sides, even within him, the bodiless fecundmellow voices of Negro women murmured. It was as though he and all other man shaped life about him had been returned to that lightness hot wet primogenitive Female".[260] In this quotation it seems that Faulkner defines Joe's reaction to Negroes as a response that is somehow associated with his dislike of women. This influence may be traced to his unpleasant, and for a child puzzling, experience with the dietitian at the orphanage and to his deception and rejection by Bobbie. Joe is frightened, and he begins to run: "That's all I wanted. That dont seem like a whole lot to ask".[261]

The use of the past tense in this quotation is a means of understanding the significance of his walk through the Negro community. From this point on Joe begins to speak and act as if his life has ended, as if he agrees with Miss Burden that it would be better if he were dead.

When Joe is leaving Freedman Town, he encounters a group of Negroes.

[258] *Ibid.*, p. 212.
[259] *Ibid.*, p. 107.
[260] *Ibid.*
[261] *Ibid.*, p. 241.

According to custom, they move out of his path avoiding contact with him, but instead of passing them he wanders deliberately into their group: "He could smell Negro; he could smell cheap cloth and sweat. The head of the Negro, higher than his own, seemed to stoop, out of the sky, against the sky. 'It's a white man', he said, without turning his head, quietly. 'What you want, white folks? You looking for somebody?' The voice was not threatful, neither was it servile".[262] In this encounter Joe is rejected by the Negro man who identifies him as a white person. The Negro man's question, "You looking for somebody"? is pertinent. Joe has been, perhaps still is, looking for himself. When the Negro leaves, "a cool wind blew from somewhere".[263] A cool wind is also referred to when Joe drives the Negro girl away and begins to fight with the boys whose pleasure he has spoiled. On this occasion when the cool wind comes, Joe discovers that his razor is in his hand; but it is not there because he is afraid of the Negro man. Evidently he is thinking of himself as a Negro person during this period, and he is angered when the group moves away from him and the man says that he is white. The intense emotion that is produced in Joe by this encounter shows how strong his conflicts are.

Joe also describes "the street" as cool. During the second phase with Miss Burden when he felt that he was "being sucked down into a bottomless morass", he longed for the street, thinking "I better get away from here". In his encounter with the tall Negro man his response is identical. In both cases there is an effort to evade the burden of his humanity and to avoid human responsibility.

In one of Joe's last encounters with Negroes he desecrates a Negro church service. The incident may be contrasted to Christ's driving the money changers from the temple, a cleansing process. One of the women who worships in the church sees Joe and thinks that he is Satan. His actions in the church are furious and diabolical. He drives the preacher from the pulpit—defiles rather than cleanses—and curses God with his hands raised in a gesture of holy exhortation. Joe drives the worshipers from the church and smashes the lamps, leaving the building disordered and dark. When this is done, he stands outside the wrecked church smoking a cigarette, visible, and offering defiance to the Negro men who were hiding in the night-darkened bushes. When he hears a mule going in the direction of town, he says: "Bound for town with the good news".[264] When Joe stands in the churchyard, "he stood lightly poised ... cool, not even breathing hard. He was quite cool, no sweat; the darkness cool upon him".[265] Usually Joe has run away from Negroes.

[262] *Ibid.*, p. 109.
[263] *Ibid.*, p. 246.
[264] *Ibid.*, p. 308.
[265] *Ibid.*, pp. 307–308.

Being in their community has been sufficient to make him restive and has filled him with a sense of urgent need to be back in the white world. This time after doing violence to the Negroes, he is able to remain "cool", and although he is surrounded by Negroes, he does not feel that he is. There is, therefore, an ambiguity in the "Bound for town with the good news". Understood to mean that the sheriff is to be told where he is, it can be interpreted as meaning that Joe says this with a cold irony. In the sense that the need for him to struggle against Negroes is mastered, for Joe, it is good news.

Joe's last contact with Negroes is not seen. He exchanges shoes with a Negro woman who is wearing her husband's brogans: "He paused to lace up the brogans: the black shoes smelling of Negro. They looked like they had been chopped out of iron ore with a dull axe. Looking down at the harsh crude, clumsy shapelessness of them he said "Hah" through his teeth".[266] These shoes and the chase whose object he is make him feel that he is "being hunted by whitemen at last into the black abyss which had been waiting, trying, for thirty years to drown him and into which now and at last he had actually entered, bearing now upon his ankles, the definite and ineradicable gauge of its upward moving".[267] Thus the shoes are not only a means of putting the dogs off his track, but they are as well a symbol of the end of his struggle against being a Negro. It is after he wears the shoes that he discovers the peace that can be found in Nature: "The air inbreathed, is like spring water. He breathes deep and slow, feeling with each breath himself diffuse in the neutral grayness, becoming one with loneliness and quiet that has never known fury and despair".[268] He thinks that this is all he has ever wanted; what he has searched for the past thirty years.

In articles published in special Faulkner issues of *Perspective* Harry M. Campbell and Phyllis Hirshleifer adequately discuss the structure of *Light in August* and agree that the plot of the novel has a thematic unity. This unity aids in the development of the reader's understanding of Joe Christmas's character.[269] Dr. Campbell says, "There is only one theme with variations: the brooding, self-conscious, introverted life imposed by modern civilization on both Joe and Hightower, as contrasted with the simple normal virtues of a life close to nature like that of Lena and (after some involvement in the chaos of civilization) Byron".[270] The life imposed by civilization upon Joe is somehow given meaning by the connotative force of the word Negro.

[266] *Ibid.*, p. 313.
[267] *Ibid.*
[268] *Ibid.*
[269] Harry M. Campbell, "Structural Devices in the Works of William Faulkner", *Perspective*, III (Autumn 1950), 225-226.
[270] *Ibid.*, p. 214.

Tone is a central device in establishing the quality of Joe's character. Faulkner describes him realistically through careful photographic details. His photograph is not distorted, but it appears larger than life size. This larger-than-life appearance comes from Faulkner's attitude toward the character and is primarily a matter of tone. Joe is frequently described as a big man walking along an empty street. Actually he does not walk along the street, but instead he moves along it with great urgency. His characteristics are those of the possessed man that are noticeable in Rider, the slave in "Red Leaves", Sutpen, and other Faulkner characters.

The Christ-parallels that form a considerable portion of the novel's imagery are too numerous to be accidental or coincidental. Joe's name is Joseph Christmas. He was found on the steps of the orphanage on Christmas day. A large part of his life is fairly anonymous. The three-year period of Christ's mission corresponds in time to the three phases of Joe's relation with Miss Burden. The last phase of this relationship may be loosely compared with the pre-Easter events. Miss Hirshleifer sees the three years with Miss Burden as representing the crucial three days, beginning with Good Friday, in Christ's life.[271] Sometimes the parallelism is in direct contrast. The triumphal entry into Jerusalem is paralleled in Joe's life with Joe's beginning of his effort to escape the Mob. Where Christ cleanses the temple, Joe desecrates it. Joe's death resembles the death of Christ. Richard Chase points out that Mrs. McEachern washes Joe's feet, that Burch betrays Joe for money (that he does not get), and Hines, his grandfather, imagines himself to be God.[272] Miss Hirshleifer points to many other parallels and calls attention to the "dominating religious motif" of the imagery.[273] Most Faulkner critics notice and comment upon the Christ-parallels since they are too numerous to be accidental. They help establish tone, by contributing to Joe's larger-than-life stature, to a realization of his suffering, to the impression that he is a possessed person, and to the recognition of his isolation. They also contribute to the metaphorical interpretation of Joe as Everyman.

Essentially the comparisons and contrasts of Joe and Christ are paradoxical. Christ bore the burden of his humanity. This emphasizes, by contrast, Joe's failure as a human being. Christ is also a symbol of love, a symbol of proper love relationships. Joe's life is a continual perversion of love relationships. Joe's life is a struggle against the affirmation of the brotherhood of man. Christ's life affirms that brotherhood. Joe's modernism contradicts the holistic concepts that cluster around the figure of Christ.

With Joe as with many other characters, Faulkner makes things symbolic

[271] Hirshleifer, pp. 235–237.
[272] Chase, p. 547.
[273] Hirshleifer, p. 235.

of the nature and personality of the individual. Joe habitually wears black and white clothes. The clothes are not only symbols of the racial conflict, but the mark of Joe as a city man. He carries a razor. In stereotyped accounts of Negro life razors are carried by Negro men for defense purposes. Joe's razor is normally associated with shaving. But in Freedman Town he holds the razor as if it was a weapon while he talks to the Negro man. Thus, the razor is made to symbolize the dual aspect of Joe's personality. The Negro shoes are the means of Joe's continuing his escape until he is ready to be captured. They are also made a part of his acceptance of his plight. When he goes into Mottstown, he continues to wear them and does not buy new ones.

The seven-day period of flight and pursuit that begins when Joe frightens the couple into driving him away from the scene of his crime is a period of self-discovery. It may be compared in its effect upon him to Christ's suffering and prayer in the garden. Joe knows that he must die. He realizes that Miss Burden was right, that he must die, when he examines the chamber of her gun after he has killed her. His flight is not an effort to escape death. Before he can die, he must be able to accept himself, and to reject those values that dominated and perverted his instincts while he was in "the street". Faulkner shows how he accomplishes this through his relations with Negroes while his flight is in progress. It is also revealed in his rejection of the physical world that has provided his escape from himself. The murder of Miss Burden is symbolic of this. Joe's appetites are stressed as a means of indicating the nature of his aberrations. Not only does he lose his desire for women, but he also loses any desire for food. Most of the women he associated with fed him. As a child the discovery of the taste of toothpaste involved him, disastrously, in the life of the dietitian. Mrs. McEachern, Bobbie, and Miss Burden fed him. During the seven days of his flight he loses his need for food. First he discovers that he has no appetite. After this discovery he forces himself to eat because of his knowledge of the body's need for food. Then he discovers that he has no need for food, that physically and mentally he is content without it.

The pattern of Joe's flight and his knowledge and acceptance of death provide for the understanding of his character in the same way that the flight of the Negro body servant in "Red Leaves" provides these understandings. Like the body-servant, when he discovered that he could not drink water, Joe recognizes when he no longer needs to eat that he has left the world of the living, and the peace that descends upon him is to be only briefly disturbed once more before his death. The quality of that peace, the imperviousness of self-acceptance, is made explicit in Joe's behavior in Mottstown, when he is a man, neither white nor black. At this time he does not respond to the compulsive force of the connotations of Negro. His conscience during this period is holistic, and his humanity is affirmed. Essentially, this is the climax of Joe's development as a character. At this point Joe may be compared to the Christ who is willing to drink his cup and Who as He emerges from the garden symbolizes the acceptance of the burden of humanity. The effect of Joe's personality upon those who saw him at this time is comparable to the effect of his appearance as he died upon those who saw him bleeding and dying in Hightower's kitchen.

The other actions of the novel that include Joe seem to me to be a final investigation of the connotative values and compulsive force of the word Negro, a final description of the "theatring" of evil. Primarily, this section of the novel exploits the responses of the people in Mottstown and Jefferson to the concept that Joe represents. The concept that Joe represents is in contrast to the thing that Joe is. Joe's grandparents, for example, accept Joe in two different ways. For old man Hines, whose code of racial superiority has driven him to depravity, Joe is the symbol of diabolism, all that is evil, and should be lynched. For Mrs. Hines he is her grandson, an extension of her flesh and personality. For the man who captured Joe in Mottstown, he was a "nigger" who killed a white woman in Jefferson. Negro is not primarily a denotative label for any of these people.

The compulsive nature of the code and the particular manner of its operation are illustrated when the people of Mottstown turn Joe over to the people of Jefferson for the administration of "justice". This axiom of social behavior is mentioned in *Intruder in the Dust* and in "Pantaloon in Black". The men of Beat Four are expected to "take care of" Lucas just as the nightwatchman's family is expected to take care of Rider. Actually the manner of complying with the code is almost formalized ritual similar to the scene in "Red Leaves", where Ikemotubbe is seen giving ritual chase to his father's body servant. In this respect Percy Grimm's part in Joe's death is ritualistic. In Grimm, respect for the legal machinery of the state and for the social conventions of the region are blended in a chauvinistic and fantastic intensity. From his point of view his actions, the mutilation and murder of Joe, represent the faithful fulfilment of a sacred duty. Faulkner emphasizes this: " 'Jesus Christ'! Grimm cried, his young voice clear and outraged like that of a young priest. 'Has every preacher [Hightower who attempted to give Joe sanctuary in his home was a preacher] and old maid in Jefferson taken down their pants to the yellowbellied son of a bitch?' "[274] Grimm is a kind of priest who defends his code. When the men of the town follow him into Hightower's kitchen and find Joe dying from his attack, Grimm stands above him saying, "Now you'll let white women alone, even in hell".[275]

In *Absalom, Absalom!* the connotative meaning of the word Negro is also explored. Quentin Compson, a Southerner, son of an aristocratic but decaying family, and a Harvard University student, reconstructs the story of Sutpen for his friend and roommate. The friend is an "outsider", and through the story Quentin attempts to make clear to him what the South is. Quentin must reconstruct the story from bare outlines. A part of it was told to him by Miss Rosa Coldfield, and he saw Jim Bond, the last of Sutpen's descendants, run from the decaying Sutpen mansion. On the eve of his going to Harvard his father told him part of the story; and while he was at Harvard, the father wrote him other parts of it in letters. Quentin fits the pieces of the story together and tries to understand its meaning as a whole. The attitude shown in the novel toward miscegenation is Quentin's. Its penetration and focus are influenced by the presence of Shreve, the roommate, who does not understand or share the South's attitude toward race.

Faulkner shows in several ways that racial differences are superficial: Thomas Sutpen realizes this and affirms it in his personal relations with his slaves. The life of the slave and that of the white man are compared as a means of establishing Henry Sutpen's character; as a result, we are given an understanding of Faulkner's attitude toward racial differences. This understanding is repeated through Miss Rosa Coldfield's encounter with Clytie on the day that Charles Bon was murdered. Rosa says that all of the barriers of race disappear when flesh touches flesh. She says this when Clytie restrains her from an act by placing her hand upon her.

Quentin seems to be aware that Sutpen knew, even when he was a boy back in Virginia, the true nature of race and that his actions in racial situations were not determined by this knowledge, but by a particular code that Sutpen chose to employ because it was a means of achieving an end that he desired. Faulkner considers slavery evil, but he does not consider Sutpen's sex relations with Negro women evil.[276] Evil, however, does grow from these relationships when Sutpen fails to assume a proper responsibility for his actions. It is his failure to assume a responsibility for Charles Bon, his son, and Charles's mother that leads to Sutpen's ruin. It is true that Sutpen had thought Charles's mother to be white when he married her. Perhaps she had deceived him, but the boy born of their union had no part in the deception and should not have been made to suffer for it. When Sutpen put this wife and child away, in response to the compulsive force of the connotations of Negro, he was

[275] *Ibid.*
[276] Cowley, Introduction, *The Portable Faulkner*, p. 16.

attempting to evade his human responsibility. Quentin knows this, and he recreates the life and purposes of Sutpen's Negro offspring with these qualifications in mind.

Charles Bon's problem, as Quentin sees it, is not primarily a problem of race. It is the problem of a rejected son. Charles knows why he is rejected, and he does not want public acknowledgment of his relation to Sutpen. Charles lives as a white man and lives without the internal conflict that characterized the life of his son and the life of Joe Christmas. He calls his wife, an octoroon joined to him by a morganatic ceremony, and his child niggers, but he refuses to deny or reject them. Although his problem is not racial, he realizes that Sutpen's and Henry's problems are, and that he must take advantage of Sutpen's racial fears to gain either recognition by his father or revenge upon the father for failure to recognize him. For this reason he tells Henry, his half-brother and Sutpen's son by the white woman whom he married after putting Charles's mother away, "I'm the nigger who's going to sleep with your sister".[277]

Faulkner uses Charles's explanation of the practice of morganatic marriage as it existed in New Orleans as one means of expressing an attitude toward miscegenation. Charles says that with the pattern of bi-racial living existing as it did in the South, miscegenation was impossible to avoid. He defends his morganatic marriage as the most humane means of participating in something that he could not avoid being a part of. Charles's point of view was an essentially different cultural attitude from that of Henry. Henry's point of view is Puritan and narrow, while Charles's is Catholic in the sense of both meanings of the word. Charles recognizes this difference and attempts to explain it to Henry. His explanation shows an understanding of the connotative value of the term Negro.

The weakness in Charles Bon's argument is that it is not a correction of an evil, but a way of accepting an essentially evil situation, perhaps a kind of amelioration. The weakness of Charles's argument, the evil of it, is reflected in his son. In a legal sense this weakness is that morganatic marriage did not provide for children, although they were legitimate, to inherit property from their fathers. Charles's death left his son practically defenseless.

Charles's son suffered the consequences of his father's sins. Faulkner takes Etienne, Charles's son, out of the Catholic world of New Orleans where it can be assumed that he would have had no racial problems and brings him into the Puritan world of Jefferson. Significantly the twelve-year-old child who is brought by Clytie to live with his paternal aunts, one white and one Negro, in Sutpen's already destroyed Hundred does not speak English. He is

[277] *Absalom, Absalom!*, p. 315.

a child who has no consciousness of race. Because of his language barrier and his youth he must sense, rather than know, the ambiguity of his relation to the two women who are his aunts. Faulkner explains the ambiguity of his life illustratively through his treatment by the two aunts, Clytie and Judith. When he comes as a child of eight with his mother to visit Sutpen's Hundred and to mourn at his father's grave, Clytie treats him as if he were a white child and refuses to allow him to play with Negro children. Clytie's behavior is significant. A white child whose blood was not mixed would have been allowed to play with a Negro. Clytie seems to fear that Etienne may discover that he is not white by playing with a Negro. Four years later, when Clytie goes to New Orleans and brings the orphaned boy to live with Judith and herself, she covers his fine silk clothes with a coarse denim jumper, a garment usually worn by Negroes. The jumper hides the clothes that symbolize the child's whiteness. Clytie is perhaps unaware of this, but it is at this point that Etienne's Negro existence begins.

At the Hundred Etienne sleeps in the same room with Judith and Clytie. Faulkner shows the reluctant and the gradual recognition of the two women of the fact that Etienne must be a Negro when his bed is removed from their room to the hallway, and finally to the isolation of the attic. By this time the clothes that were a symbol of his whiteness, or at least a protection against being a Negro, are outgrown rags that hang in his closet and the child has begun to realize that there is something about him that makes him different from other people. This realization Faulkner illustrates with the broken shard of mirror that the child hides in his room and peers into surreptitiously trying to discover in his face some evidence of the thing that makes him different.

During this period of childhood and adolescence Clytie and Judith keep him isolated from other people, but they give him no explanations. Faulkner does not describe the boy's mastery of the English language, but the experiences he had at the Hundred must certainly have conditioned the meaning of the word Negro for him in such a way that the connotative values of the word were far greater than its denotative values.

Etienne's adolescent years are a period in which he searches for knowledge of himself much as Joe Christmas does. And although there are facts that would enable him to know who and what he is biologically and socially, Clytie and Judith hide these facts from him until he has begun a pattern of violent living comparable to that of Joe Christmas's pilgrimage in "the street". Because he does not discover that Clytie and Judith are his aunts until he has established his pattern of living, we are given another instance, as in Joe Christmas, of the compulsive force of the connotative values of the word Negro. There is a compulsion that forces Etienne to seek violence in the same way that Joe Christmas sought it. His conflict, like Joe's, is a mental one. Like his father he could have been white if he had wanted to be. After his first violent outbreak he was given money by Judge Compson and told to go away. "You can be whatever you will", Judge Compson told him. He returned to Jefferson with "a coal black and ape-like woman and an authentic wedding license" and continued a life characterized by his deliberate search for violent encounter.[278] The woman, "the black gargoyle", is not used as Joe's common-law wife was. She is, rather, a means of inciting the antagonism of white and Negro men. "The man apparently hunted out situations in order to flaunt and fling the ape-like body of his charcoal companion in the faces of all who would retaliate".[279] They appeared to represent the marriage of a Negro woman and a white man. What they actually were most people who came in contact with Etienne did not try to discover.

A further and useful understanding of Faulkner's handling of miscegenation can be found in "Delta Autumn", one of the stories from *Go Down, Moses*. "Delta Autumn" is an analysis of a social problem. It does not seek primarily to reveal character. The situation poses the question of what is to be done when a white man and a Negro woman are in love. The two people in this story are in love. The woman returns to the scene of her first meeting with Roth Edmonds because she thinks there is a possibility of continuing their relationship or of gaining some parting assurance of a love that exists although it must be renounced. Perhaps she even has hopes of marriage. Faulkner does not say what she expected; but when Isaac gives her the money that Roth had left for her, she says: "That's just money".

Faulkner's method in this story is that of understatement. It is not perfectly clear until near the end of the story that the woman who is being talked about is Negro. Legate suggests this by saying that she is light-colored and that Roth had been going coon-hunting, but Uncle Isaac does not know until he discovers the woman's relationship to his own family. For a time it is not clear that a woman is being talked about at all. The men are restive and the tone that is supplied by the coarse bantering of Legate gives their restiveness intensity. The subject about which they talk is so serious that it cannot be talked about in an open way. When Uncle Isaac and the woman talk in the second half of the story, indirection is still used. The method reveals the serious and the complex nature of the problem.

Roth Edmonds had begun the affair with the woman a year before while he was at the annual hunting camp. The two of them had gone to New Mexico

[278] *Ibid.*, p. 204.
[279] *Ibid.*, pp. 205–206.

and lived together for a short time, and then Roth had left the woman. They had written to each other. He had sent her money, and she had had a child by him. As the group of men drive up to the camp for the annual deer hunt, Roth thinks about his problem. He knows that he is going to meet the woman again and that he must decide what he will do. The men who are with him know about the woman; and while they drive to camp, they tease Roth by saying that he hunted a doe the year before, and they speculate about what he will hunt during this season.

Isaac McCaslin places the affair in an ethical framework. Isaac does not allow the cavalier jest that women and children "are two things this world ain't ever lacked" to go unanswered.[280] Isaac says that this is just "the mind's reason a man has to give himself because the heart don't always have time to bother with thinking up words that fit together".[281] Following this, Isaac states an attitude toward man's actions. Man acts, Isaac suggests, to satisfy his urges, and he thinks afterwards. The product of his thinking is a kind of self-exculpation in which "good" reasons are substituted for "real" reasons. Isaac interprets man's actions from the point of view of man's nature:

God created man and He created the world for him to live in and I reckon He created the kind of world He would have wanted to live in if he had been a man and maybe He didn't put the desire to hunt and kill game [the woman Roth was in love with is referred to constantly as a doe] in man but I reckon He knew it was going to be there, that man was going to teach it to himself, since he wasn't God himself yet —.[282]

Isaac suggests that there are consequences of the hunting. Of man he says, "The woods and fields he ravages and the game he devastates will be the consequence and signature of his crime and guilt, and punishment".[283] The "hunting" that man does is therefore of serious importance and not merely a matter to be made a jest of by a man's friends. Isaac says that love relation-ships are sacred: "I think that every man and woman, at the instant when it dont even matter whether they marry or not, I think that whether they marry then or afterward or dont never, at that instant the two of them together were God".[284] The sacred nature of love relationships is not accepted by Roth. He says to Isaac: "Then there are some Gods in this world I wouldn't want to touch, and with a damn long stick. . . . And that includes myself". There is active in Roth's conscious evaluation of his acts the Puritanism that Charles Bon sees in Henry Sutpen. Roth is influenced by the prevailing social

---

[280] "Delta Autumn", *Go Down, Moses*, p. 348.
[281] *Ibid.*
[282] *Ibid.*, p. 348.
[283] *Ibid.*, p. 349.
[284] *Ibid.*, p. 348.

attitude to the relation that he has been involved in. He finds it profane in spite of the necessity he found to enter it.

During the ride to the camp Roth is tense and nervous, and the reader can understand that he is trying to decide what to do about the woman. Before the time came to leave for camp, he had decided not to go. When he is driving up, he stops the car several times as if he would like to go back. At the camp he does not have the courage to tell the woman that he is ending their affair. Perhaps this means that he is afraid of the response that he would make to her if he met her face to face. He leaves camp before she comes and gives Isaac the task of dealing with her.

Legate states Roth's problem as it is looked upon by the white people of his community:

Oh, Roth's coming. . . . If it was just a buck he was coming all this distance for, now. But he's got a doe in here. Of course a old man like Uncle Ike cant be interested in no doe, not one that walks on two legs — when she's standing up, that is. Pretty light-colored, too. The one he was after them nights last fall when he said he was coon-hunting, Uncle Ike. The one I figured maybe he was still running when he was gone all that month last January.[285]

According to the prevailing social attitudes it is acceptable for white men to use Negro women for their pleasure. Legate does not condemn Roth. There is perhaps a tone of praise in his bantering jocularity. He treats the woman as if she were an animal to be hunted like any other game. He does not see the relationship as one involving sacred human responsibilities.

"Delta Autumn" takes place just before the United States entered the second World War. Because of the certainty of war when Roth says, "I'm going in. . . . This will be the last of it", his meaning is mistaken. Legate takes advantage of the ambiguity of the statement to make another jest, and then the men begin to discuss the purpose of war. Isaac says the only fighting anywhere that ever had anything of God's blessing "has been when men fought to protect does and fawns".[286] Roth answers that there is never a scarcity of women and children. In Roth there is a conflict between the things he wants to do and what society says he must do. Roth says that men were better when Isaac was young. But Isaac answers "There are good men everywhere, at all times", and that he had known some "that even circumstances couldn't stop".[287] Roth has been challenged by circumstances. Perhaps this speech by Isaac is meant to suggest a course of action to him, a course of action that he would not have suggested had he known the woman was a Negro. But it seems

[285] *Ibid.*, p. 337.
[286] *Ibid.*, p. 339.
[287] *Ibid.*, p. 345.

that Roth prefers to accept the point of view "That it's only because folks happen to be watching him that a man behaves at all".[288] If this is true, it is also likely to be true that a man will behave as the watchers expect or demand him to behave. The watchers make and define the circumstances. Roth does not have the courage to defy the "folks" who are watching. He does not have the courage to break with convention and to adjust his relation with the woman as he wants it to be.

Isaac's talk with the Negro woman is divided into two parts. In the first of these he does not know that she is a Negro. What he says to her then is what might be said to any woman who has gone far enough with a man to have a child by him, before she attempted to discover whether or not he was going to marry her. The woman had not expected marriage. She said, "I knew that to begin with, long before honor I imagine he called it told him the time had come to tell me in so many words that his code I suppose he would call it would forbid him forever to do". After this she not only tells Isaac that she is a Negro but she explains to him that she is a member of his own family.

When Isaac knows that the woman is a Negro, *"Maybe in a thousand or two years in America* he thought. *But not now! Not now!* He cried, not loud, in a voice of amazement, pity and outrage: 'You're a nigger' "![289] His reaction to the knowledge that the woman is a Negro expresses Faulkner's attitude that time will be needed to correct the evils of the South. Isaac knows that miscegenation exists as a social fact and that it must be recognized, but as a legal condition solemnized by marriage, although it will come, it cannot come for many years. This is the point of view of the gradualist. It is of some significance that this response comes from Isaac. He is one of Faulkner's "good" characters, whose life has been devoted to justice and right living. And yet when he is faced with the possibility of a white man marrying a Negro woman, he expresses "amazement, pity, and outrage".

Perhaps he feels all of these things because he does not understand. At least he does not understand the woman's motivation. "Marry a black man", he tells her. "You are young, handsome, almost white; you could find a black man who would see in you what it was you saw in him, who would ask nothing of you and expect less and get still less than that, if it's revenge you want".[290] And then the woman makes clear what her motivation is. She loves Roth Edmonds. It is on this note that Faulkner ends the discussion. Perhaps in this situation Isaac surrenders to the connotative values of Negro. Significantly, when he gives the woman the money Roth left for her she says:

[288] *Ibid.*, p. 346.
[289] *Ibid.*, p. 361.
[290] *Ibid.*

"that's only money". When Isaac tells her to marry a man of her race, she tells him she is in love with Roth. By contrast her morality is higher than Isaac's. The money represents the conventional way of ending relationships of the kind that she is involved in. The woman "thrust the money into the slicker's side pocket as if it were a soiled handkerchief".[291] The gesture is an evaluation of the convention.

As a youth, when Isaac attempted to discover why the Negro woman whose daughter had been wronged by his grandfather committed suicide, he came to the conclusion that love was involved. He decided that the woman loved her daughter, and that perhaps she still loved old Carothers, who had been her first lover. He was not satisfied to predicate Carothers's relation with the girl on lust. He struggled to believe that Carothers had loved the girl. A part of the significance in "Delta Autumn", therefore, seems to be the fact that Isaac has lost some of his acute awareness of the nature of human relations. He places Roth's relation with the woman in an ethical framework before he knows that she is a Negro; but when he discovers that she is not white, he does not apply his ethical analysis in judging her case. He shifts his point of view. Previously he has condemned Roth's refusal to assume full responsibility for his actions. Upon the discovery that the woman is a Negro, he stops his censure and begins to examine the situation from a point of view of its origin and its social framework. Although he does not state his approval of Roth's decision, he does not find it possible that Roth can act in any other way. Isaac responds, more or less, as society would expect him to. For this reason the woman's morality may be said to be higher than his.

The woman came to see Roth because she loved him, not because she expected him to marry her. The consistency of Isaac as a point-of-view character is weakened when he fails to recognize this. His failure of sensibility in this instance reveals the complexity of the problem that Faulkner is dealing with in this story. If Isaac is bewildered by it, no one in the Faulkner world can be expected to see it steadily and as a whole. The cumulative force of convention triumphs over Isaac's human impulses.

When the woman tells him who she is, of her kinship to his family, he is moved. He touches her hand, a gesture significant of the emotional impact of the moment: "He didn't grasp it, he merely touched it — the gnarled, bloodless, bone-light bone dry old man's fingers touching for a second the smooth young flesh where the strong old blood ran after its long journey back to home".[292] For the child, he gives her the hunting horn that General Compson had left him in his will, an act of recognition and significant generosity; but he recoils when she says "yes" to him. It is while he is emotionally disturbed by her "yes" that he tells her to marry a black man and assumes that she was attracted to Roth because he was white. He tells her: "You can find a black man who would see in you what it was you saw in him, who would ask nothing of you and expect less and get even still less than that".[293] This is a variant expression of the idea that all Negro men desire white women. And when Isaac states it, Faulkner shows the extent to which even Isaac is controlled by his social world.

At the end of the story Faulkner shifts from the particular to the general. Through Isaac's thinking, the woman's problem is shown to be a result of the twin evils. "No wonder the ruined woods I used to know don't cry for retribution! He thought: The people who have destroyed it will accomplish its revenge".[294] While he is still thinking, Legate comes in and says that Roth has shot a deer. Isaac says it was a doe, shifting Legate's meaning from the animal world of the hunt to the area of human relations and continuing his thinking about the evil that he had begun before Legate entered the tent. The denuded forests, a reminder of man's effort to possess the land, claim as a part of their revenge the failure of Roth and the woman he loves to be able to make a life of their own.

IV

Lionel Trilling suggests that the most distinctive characteristic of Faulkner's morality is its almost religious respect for the pieties.[295] The group of faithful women servants, Dilsey, Elnora, and Clytie, exhibit this characteristic morality. They have honor, pride and dignity. They are simple, strong, courageous, stoical, unlettered, and untroubled by sex aberrations. They are, in fact, a vanished class. Faulkner's revelation of their character may, indeed, be called a memorial to the Negro servant. As Faulkner says of Dilsey, it may be said that each of these women endured.

To endure is to bear the burden of one's humanity, frequently without hope or compensation. Each of these women identifies herself with a particular white family and its fortunes and works as hard as she can to protect the family and its honor. The women are generally contrasts to the families they serve. The Sartorises, Sutpens, and Compsons are destroyed. These women who serve them survive. As a group they have integrated a body of experiences and have derived from them a core of moral truth.

Dilsey's character is revealed through a description of one' day of her life

[293] *Ibid.*, p. 263.
[294] *Ibid.*, p. 364.
[295] Trilling, pp. 205–207.

as the Compson servant. Significantly this day is Easter Sunday, and the events that occur in it form the fourth and concluding section of *The Sound and the Fury*. Through the things that Dilsey does, we see that she has two loyalties, one to man and one to God, and that the second makes the first possible.

Before Dilsey goes to church on this particular Sunday, she deals with the wants and frustrations that are characteristic identifications of the Compson family's decay. Mrs. Compson wants her hot water bottle filled. Jason must not be awakened by the noise of Benjy's dressing or by his idiot tantrums. Luster's mischievousness must be kept in hand and guided to help her prepare and serve breakfast. Jason must not be allowed to hurt Quentin. The quality of Dilsey's daily living is revealed through her effort to satisfy the Compson wants and needs. On this particular Sunday morning one of the family's major calamities is discovered. Jason discovers that his niece Quentin has stolen his savings and has run away with a circus performer. Mrs. Compson and he are thoroughly disturbed, but Dilsey is calm and placating, protecting them from each other and trying to preserve the routine of daily living and function. "Go and eat yo breakfast", she says to Jason.[296] Dilsey is a kind of chorus in this Easter drama of the Compson's lives. Her loyalty has crystallized into habit, but she does not become involved emotionally in the Compson tantrums. In contrast to the family she is strong.

Her strength is shown in her ability to remain remarkably unperturbed through all of the family emergencies that beset the Compsons, to keep her poise, dignity, and sense of order. Her reactions to the incidents of daily living reveal the unity of her character, and evidence of strength, in contrast to the lack of emotional control in those members of the Compson family who surround her. The events of daily living show her ability to adjust to circumstances; and even though she is unable to change them, perhaps to understand them, to keep herself intact.

Characteristically, Dilsey displays this ability at the beginning of the novel's fourth section. Because it is Sunday she dresses for church before going into the Compson kitchen. When she comes to the door of her cabin, she discovers that it is raining. She must change her clothes to prevent the rain from spoiling them. Her face expresses fatalism and "a child's disappointment", but she withdraws into her cabin and changes into clothes that will not be harmed and then goes to do her work. In appreciation of her Evelyn Scott says: "But there is Dilsey . . . stoic as some immemorial carving of heroism, going on, doing the best she can guided only by instinct and affection and the self-respect she will not relinquish — the ideal of herself to

---

[296] William Faulkner, *The Sound and the Fury* (New York, 1929), p. 305.

which she conforms irrationally, which makes of her life something whole, while her 'white folks' accept their fragmentary state, disintegrate".[297]

Dilsey's Christian faith is the source of her strength. The nature of this faith is indicated in her reactions to the visiting minister, a most unprepossessing person. Dilsey says of him: "I've knowed de Lawd to use cuiser tools dan dat".[298] The minister is a tool for Dilsey. At the beginning of his sermon he announces, "I got the recollection and the blood of the Lamb!"[299] And Dilsey sat "bolt upright" with her hand on Benjy's knee and "two tears slid down her fallen cheeks, in and out of the myriad coruscations of immolation and abnegation and time".[300] She cries because she also has a recollection. Faulkner says she cried "in the annealment and the blood of the remembered Lamb".[301] Sumner C. Powell in an essay in *Perspective* stresses this point and reminds his reader that "Dilsey tells Caddy [one of the Compson children] she knows her name is 'Dilsey' because it has long been 'writ out' in the Lord's Book, to be read by the angels".[302]

Benjy's presence beside Dilsey in church indicates that her faith is not separate from her daily living. It also indicates her disregard of what other people may choose to say about her. People criticize her for taking the idiot Benjy to church with her, but she ignores this criticism. "Tell them", she says, "de good Lawd don't keer whether he smart or not. Don't nobody but white trash keer".[303] The nature of Dilsey's religious experience was determined by her life with the Compsons. Her comment to Frony, her daughter, "I've seed de first en de last", indicates this. The phrase indicates the union of Dilsey's religious and social life, for she uses the language of the book of *Revelations* to state her critical observation of the Compson family. Her participation in the symbolic sufferings of Christ through the suggestive cadence and pattern of the minister's sermon gives her the courage to face adequately the truth about the Compson family which she has made the center and purpose of her life.

The decay of the Sartoris family is not as repulsive in its details as that of the Compson and Sutpen families. As individuals they retain more human dignity than do the Compsons. While the Compsons become morally decadent and degenerate, the Sartorises become, though they do not lose their morality, morally ineffective. The world they are forced to live in is one in which their principles can no longer be made the basis of effective action. The difference

[297] Evelyn Scott, *On William Faulkner's The Sound and the Fury* (New York, 1929), p. 10.
[298] *The Sound and the Fury*, p. 309.
[299] *Ibid.*, p. 310.
[300] *Ibid.*, p. 311.
[301] *Ibid.*, p. 313.
[302] Sumner C. Powell, "William Faulkner Celebrates Easter, 1928", *Perspective*, II (Summer 1949), 213.
[303] *The Sound and the Fury*, p. 320.

between these two families is made clear through the ways in which Elnora and Dilsey differ.

Elnora is a Sartoris in a sense that Dilsey is not a Compson. This is especially true of Elnora in "There Was a Queen". Elnora is the elder Bayard Sartoris's half-sister, and her point of view is the Sartoris point of view. Like that of the Sartoris family, her way of life has been encroached upon and she as an individual is being defeated. When the story takes place, her husband Caspey is in jail for stealing; and Jobey, her son, has gone to Memphis to wear fine clothes on Beale Street.[304] Nevertheless, she clings to the Sartoris ideals; and as Faulkner uses her in this story, she is a point-of-view character.

Her perception and statement of the Sartoris point of view is clear and rationally conceived in contrast to Dilsey's "irrational" achievement of a unified way of life. Through her Faulkner explicitly defines quality. "Born Sartoris or born quality of any kind aint *is*, it's *does*".[305] This statement is a judgment of Narcissa Benbow, the widow of Young Bayard Sartoris. When the story opens, only two lineal descendants of the Sartoris family are left alive, Old Miss Jenny and her great great nephew Bory, who is Narcissa's son. Elnora judges Narcissa because she went away to Memphis, leaving her child and Miss Jenny alone for several days without a proper regard for decorum. Narcissa comes from a family whose name is "good", but Elnora says that the conditions of her birth are not sufficient to make her a person of quality. "She won't never be a Sartoris woman; because her actions are not the actions of Sartoris women".[306] Here Sartoris is defined as O'Donnell suggests as the polar opposite of Snopes. Narcissa has gone to Memphis because of letters that were written to her by a Snopes, and her behavior is comparable to Snopes behavior.

Elnora is not only able to judge Narcissa's behavior accurately, she is also able to isolate the weakness of Sartoris morality: "I knowed what she was up to all the time. Because I knows trash. I knows the way trash goes about working in with quality. Quality can't see that, because its quality. But I can".[307] This acuteness of understanding, perhaps, is greater than Dilsey's "I've seed de first en de last". Elnora has not only judged Narcissa, but she has isolated the cause of the failure of Sartoris morality. As Cowley suggests, the Sartoris morality fails because it has no defense against its enemies. To combat the Snopeses one must act as Snopeses act. And if actions are indications of quality, in order to defeat the Snopeses one must cease to be Sartoris.

[304] "There Was a Queen", p. 99.
[305] *Ibid.*, p. 105.
[306] *Ibid.*, p. 102.
[307] *Ibid.*, p. 107.

Elnora's ability to isolate the weakness of Sartoris morality is evidence of the strength of her character. She knows like Dilsey that her allegiance is given to a lost cause. When her knowledge is related to her behavior, the remarkable aspect of her character is established. She has respect for the pieties and a respect for tradition.

Elnora chose to serve Miss Jenny and Bory, and through service to them to show a proper respect for the pieties, not because she wanted to make them comfortable, but because she respected the past that they represented: "It ain't Bory's needings and it ain't her needings. It's dead folks needings. Old Marse John's and Cunnels and Mister Johns and Bayards that dead and can't do nothing about it. That's where the needings is. That's what I'm talking about".[308] This sense of responsibility to one's ancestors, while it is not a religious sentiment, has the quality of religious faithfulness and is essentially a pious attitude. Elnora assumes this responsibility. "I can take care of her. I don't need no help", she says when she realizes that Narcissa cannot be depended upon to behave properly toward Old Miss Jenny.[309]

The faithfulness of Elnora and Dilsey is found again in *Absalom* in Clytie. Clytie is the daughter of Sutpen and one of the two slave women he brought to his Hundred in 1833. As is true of Dilsey and Elnora, we do not become aware of her quality until the destruction of her family has begun and its doom is unmistakable. At the beginning of the war the doom of the family is predictable; and Clytie and Judith, Sutpen's legitimate daughter, are left alone to care for his home and property. They share this responsibility equally while Judith lives. After Judith's death the responsibility is entirely Clytie's. The family cannot be saved; at the most it is only possible to guard its secrets from public curiosity. The chain of calamities begins when Sutpen goes to war. His wife dies. Henry Sutpen, the heir, kills Charles Bon, his half-brother and his sister's lover. Charles Bon's son becomes an orphan and is brought by Clytie to live with and be cared for by herself and Judith. As a young man he develops a neurosis which is caused by the racial conflicts in his life, and he is constantly in trouble until his death. After Judith's death Clytie is left the whole responsibility of caring for the house and the idiot grandson of Charles Bon.

Seemingly Clytie accepts the dogma that the sins of the father are to be visited upon the children. As Sutpen's daughter she accepts it as her lot to bear and to expiate through work and suffering the burden of his sin. Her last gesture is a feeble but courageous effort to give sanctuary to the fratricide Henry Sutpen who has come home to die. "Whatever he done [Clytie says

[308] *Ibid.*
[309] *Ibid.*, p. 100.

to Quentin Compson], me and Judith and him have paid it out".[310] The "he" referred to here is Thomas Sutpen's son Henry, but it may very well be interpreted to mean Thomas himself, for his son was the instrument used to carry out a sin that he had planned. Clytie "paid out" her father's sins through hardships and suffering. During the war she cut wood, plowed, cooked, and endured privation to keep his home for him until his return from the war.

Rosa Coldfield both hated and feared Clytie because she saw in her a representative of Sutpen's interests and something of Sutpen himself. Rosa says of her that she was "firm and antedating time and house and doom and all". Clytie recognized Rosa as an outsider and as an enemy; and although she was a white woman, Clytie did not fear her. When Rosa attempted to interfere in Sutpen affairs—to take the sick Henry Sutpen into town for treatment and perhaps for punishment for his crime—Clytie sets fire to the Sutpen house and ends Henry's and her life. Her last act is one of stoic courage and determination.

V

Faulkner's definition of the Negro problem is broad and inclusive and carefully related in its perspective to the area of the country that he is writing about. In *Light in August*, he is primarily concerned with the concept of race as it affects bi-racial living in the South. In *Intruder in the Dust*, he is concerned with the problem of justice. In *Requiem for a Nun*, it is almost possible to say that Faulkner is not concerned with the problem of race, but with the problems of evil. If this were said, it should be added that the story amounts to a parable that essentially represents the ideal of Isaiah's suffering servant. Nancy was despised, rejected, and acquainted with griefs, but it is she who points the way to salvation for the Gavin Stevenses as well as for the Temple Drakes. We have in Nancy's portrait also an illustration of the moral superiority of the victim.

In general it may be said that Faulkner's Negro characters destroy the kind of myth that supports Negro stereotypes in fiction. He says that the Negro's undesirable characteristics are copied from white people and that they are an indication of formed habit rather than of racial particularity. His Negroes, though most of them are uneducated in a formal sense, are intellectually competent. Faulkner does not justify the social and economic advantages that some men take of Negroes, nor does he defend their acts on moral grounds that predicate the Negro's individuality as different from that of white men. His Negroes are human in the same ways that his white

[310] *Absalom, Absalom!*, p. 370.

characters are. His references to the Negro's choice of food, clothes, and amusement show that these are the result of habit induced by social and economic necessity.

Through Faulkner's technical approach to characterization we gain more than a surface knowledge of Negro character. He reveals character through analysis. He explains that appearances are often deceptive. Frequently, he introduces a character at a point of maturity, introduces what may seem at first glance to be a stereotype or a type character, and then by lifting away, as it were, layer after layer of the character's thought and experience, he qualifies and redefines what at first glance seemed to be the real character.

In addition to Faulkner's particular technical approach, there is also the problem of evil which assists in determining his character portraits. This essay began with an attempt to show that Faulkner believes there is a right relationship that should exist between man and nature and that the evils of man's life are derived from the perversion of this relationship. It may be said that the two evils — man's efforts to possess the land, Negro slavery, and the developments from these — are the threads from which Faulkner's Negro characters are woven. The particular concern in this essay is to study the creation of and attitudes toward Negro character. In the world of Faulkner's fiction it is not possible to do this without realizing that Negro character is the result of the two seminal evils.

In the Christian sense, at least, Faulkner writes as if man's will is free. At the same time, as the observer of a particular social scene, he sees a series of events, and in his effort to understand these events he places them in a causal pattern.

In the first place, what Faulkner says about free will and causation, implicitly and explicitly, is closely related to what he says about ancestral sin. Sin, as a matter of fact, is a causal agent in a negative sense. It deprives. Within the framework of Christian doctrine men may sin, but they may also refrain from sinning. Man's will must be free in order for certain of his acts to be classified as sins. When man has committed a sin, however, the act may have consequences. We may say, for example, that Sutpen's attitude toward the treatment of the Negro women whose bodies he had used was sinful. Sutpen chose freely. There were factors that influenced his choice, but he might have chosen otherwise. Once Sutpen's sin had been committed, a chain of events followed it that may be called its effects.

Clytie recognizes this in *Absalom, Absalom!* when she attempts to "pay for" the wrong that her father has done. Faulkner's concern with the operation of evil and the effects of evil upon his characters is similar to Hawthorne's concern with evil in the *The House of the Seven Gables*. Greed causes the

Pyncheons to deal unjustly with the Maules. Their sin is a sin of pride. In Faulkner's fiction man's effort to possess the land, materialism, may also be called a sin of pride. As it does in Hawthorne, this sin results from egotism and egoism and blinds its possessors to the sacred nature of other human personalities. The conditions that exist in *The House of the Seven Gables* when the story opens are the result of Pyncheon greed just as the conditions that exist at Sutpen's Hundred after his death may be said to be the result of Sutpen's greed.

Hawthorne's treatment of sin is relentless. The sinner must repent and confess. But what then? Is there no restoration? St. Paul, on whose writing the Puritans nourished their stark souls, made much of the Law, but he also brought good news. *The Epistle to the Romans*, his theological masterpiece, declares indeed that "by one man sin entered into the world, and death by sin; so death passed upon all men, for that all have sinned" and even that "the law entered, that the offense [of sin] might abound". Here Hawthorne stopped reading, but the Apostle went on: "But where sin abounded, grace did much more abound". Sin there was, to be sure, and through sin we became God's enemies; but through the Atonement we have "joy in God through our Lord Jesus Christ".[311]

Generally, we may say that Faulkner's exegesis of evil parallels Hawthorne's; however, Hawthorne stops at the law while Faulkner goes beyond the law to grace. Atonement is possible for Faulkner's characters as we see in the examples of Temple Drake and Isaac McCaslin. There is hope in Faulkner. His South can and will rid itself of its ancestral evils. This is the thesis of *Intruder in the Dust*.

We may examine Eugene O'Neill's *Mourning Becomes Electra* for a somewhat different concept of ancestral sin. In this play O'Neill seems to be a complete determinist and to substitute determinism for the Greek Nemesis. The play is externally a retelling of the story of Agamemnon, Clytemnestra, Orestes, and Electra in which O'Neill has reinterpreted the old doctrine of Nemesis in terms of the biological and psychological doctrine of cause and effect. In *Mourning Becomes Electra* evil, or fate, makes Orin and Lavinia what they are. At the end of the third part of the trilogy, *The Haunted*, when Lavinia realizes how things are with Orin and herself and goes into the Mannon House and closes the door behind her for the last time, we are reminded of Clytie's last act.

Lavinia's act, however, represents her failure and her recognition of her failure to be able to arrange destiny. When Clytie is last seen staring from a window on the upper floor of the burning Sutpen house, she has achieved a victory and is successfully defying the intentions of the town. In effect,

311 Austin Warren, ed., *Nathaniel Hawthorne*, AWS (New York, 1934), pp. xxxviii-xxxix.

Clytie has been able to make her destiny. We feel that Lavinia acts because powers beyond her control cause her to act. Clytie's actions are prescribed by caste and poverty; but her will is free, and her choices result from the action of a free will. Clytie acts from a sense of moral duty. Much of her acting is not acting in the sense of trying to get things done. It is rather the taking of a moral attitude toward a situation and waiting or, as Faulkner would say, enduring.

O'Neill and Aeschylus give us a source for the evil in the lives of their characters. Faulkner does also. He believes that man violated the intentions of God: Faulkner says that "He" tells in the "Book" how "He" created the earth, and created man to be "His" overseer on the earth "and to hold suzerainty over the earth and the animals in His name". Man was to hold the earth mutual and intact in the communal anonymity of brotherhood. The Indians, for example, held the land this way before they attempted to pattern their lives after those of white men. As we are told in "Red Leaves", the Indians began to have trouble when they began selling land to white men and buying Negro slaves as the white men did. If we examine the total meaning of a novel like *Sartoris* or *Absalom, Absalom!* we must recognize a violation of "His" moral directive as the factor that causes the failure of the Sartoris and Sutpen families. The evils that Faulkner defines, in fact, as causal agents are a form of materialism. He feels apparently that man is not forced, or determined, to violate God's intention in his use of the land. The violation of the land is, therefore, a free choice.

Except in the meaning that we can find in stories like "Go Down, Moses", and in a few scattered passages such as those I have used earlier in this essay, Faulkner does not say that he believes in freedom of the will. About most of man's actions, however, Faulkner seemingly wants to say man could have done otherwise. When Faulkner says that man's will is free, one of the things that he does mean is that man does not have to choose evil. Men do not have to choose as they do. They may choose otherwise. This possibility of free choice seems to be the basis of Faulkner's optimism that the South can and will correct its own evils.

Faulkner recognizes moral responsiblity and moral virtue. If the choices that man makes are to be considered the basis for judging his virtue, then he must be able to choose freely. Nancy's characterization in *Requiem for a Nun* tells us something about the relation of free will and causation in Faulkner's world. We can say that Faulkner shows us some of the things that cause Nancy to be the kind of woman that she is. Her economic security is marginal. She is a laundress in Jefferson, Mississippi, before the first World War when we meet her in "That Evening Sun". Socially her security is marginal. She can be exploited by the white women of the town and by the white men. Her own people can offer her no security. They, in fact, exploit her also. Nancy is a whore. She has drives and urges, a personality that seeks to assert itself. If fulfillment is denied her in one area, she seeks it in another. Nancy is part of a system. We can say that the operation of evil in the world makes Nancy the kind of a person she is. Nancy is however, a "nun"; and it is the exercise of her free will, her assumption of moral responsibility that makes her this. Nancy's decision to kill Temple's baby is what Faulkner would regard as a free choice. Nancy might have chosen to keep out of the affairs of white people. The consideration of the relation of evil to the development of Negro character in Faulkner's fiction gains from the discussion of the relation of free choice and the causative function of evil in Faulkner's world.

Perhaps the most distinctive thing about Faulkner's creation of Negro character is his destruction of the Negro stereotype. The stereotype is what we must call a social being. Faulkner's Negro characters are individuals. In considering the myths that are basic to Negro stereotypes, we may say that Faulkner asks certain questions that are designed to give him objective meaning. He attempts, it seems, to discover whether a particular belief about the Negro has any meaning. Through such a process he discovers what that meaning ultimately is. He next makes an attempt to discover what other statements must be pre-supposed, if the given statement is to be true. In this way he gains knowledge of his characters' world and of their relation to it. Isaac McCaslin provides a good example of this process when he attempts to discover why Lucas's paternal grandmother commits suicide. Faulkner's success in making his Negroes real people depends upon his theory of the cause and operation of evil and upon his ability to relate this social theory to the craft of fiction.

The definitive portrait of the Negro, Lucas, provides a perspective from which to observe all of Faulkner's Negro characters. In relation to the group, he is the archetypal pattern. Lucas faces most of the problems that a Negro can face in the South. Lucas makes clear the meaning and the theoretical conceptions back of the smaller and less explicitly dealt-with characters. At times he seems to be possessed; usually he is larger than life, but he always bears the burden of his humanity. Faulkner makes use of his favorite devices in developing him: the principle of undercutting, psychic distance, the image in the round. As a victim he is morally superior. He is an individual. He is simple, strong, courageous, stoical, comparatively unlettered and untroubled by sexual aberrations. He has pride and humility, honor and dignity. The favorite Faulkner adjectives may be applied to him: impervious, impenetrable, imponderable. Lucas illustrates Faulkner's meaning when he says: "Yesterday, today, tomorrow are is". These qualities of the archetypal figure are the result of his and his ancestors' effort to avoid the effects of the two evils when they could and to deal with them when they had to do so. In varying degrees the things that can be said of Lucas can be said of each of Faulkner's Negro characters.